Frontier Woman

Other Books by Walker D. Wyman

Available through the University of Wisconsin-River Falls Press
    North Hall, River Falls, Wisconsin 54022

The Wild Horse of the West (paperback, 1989)

Nothing But Prairie and Sky (paperback, 1989)

History of the Wisconsin State Universities (1968). Editor.

The Lumberjack Frontier (1968 cloth; 1976 paperback)

Mythical Creatures of the North Country (1969, 1970 paperback)

The Legend of Charley Glass (1970). Pamphlet. With J. Hart.

Centennial History of the University of Wisconsin-River Falls
    (1976). With J. King.

*The Frosting on the Cake — History of the University of
    Wisconsin-River Falls Foundation, 1948-1976* (1977)

Witching for Water, Oil, and Precious Minerals (1977, paperback)

Charles Round Low Cloud   Voice of the Winnebago
    (1979, paperback). With William Leslie Clark.

Mythical Creatures of the U.S.A. and Canada (University of
    Wisconsin-River Falls Press, 1978. Cloth, paperback.)

*Distinguished Alumni of the University of Wisconsin-River Falls,
    1959-1977* (University of Wisconsin-River Falls, 1977)

Wisconsin Folklore (1978, paperback)

Wisconsin and North Country Wolf and Bear Stories
    (1986, paperback)

Stories of Domestic Animals and Other Creatures (1986, paperback)

Wisconsin and North Country Stories About Fish and Fishermen
    (1987, paperback)

Wisconsin and North Country Stories About Hunters and Hunting
    (1987, paperback)

Frontier Woman

The Life of a Woman Homesteader

on the Dakota Frontier

Retold from the original notes and letters
of Grace Fairchild, a Wisconsin teacher,
who went to South Dakota in 1898

By Walker D. Wyman

Illustrated by Helen B. Wyman

University of Wisconsin-River Falls Press

Printed in the United States of America
By Weber & Sons, Inc., Park Falls, WI

First Printing, April 1972
Second Printing, March 1974
Third Printing, April 1978
Fourth Printing, July 1981
Fifth Printing, October 1987
Sixth Printing, June 1989
Seventh Printing, March 1990
Eighth Printing, May 1991
Ninth Printing, April 1994
Tenth Printing, September 1997

University of Wisconsin-River Falls Press
An adjunct of the University of Wisconsin-River Falls Foundation

Preface

South Dakota with its rolling plains and prairies has had a colorful history in its first 100 years. It had long been the home of several Indian tribes whose life centered on the buffalo and the horse. Fur traders found their way to this country after the 1740s, but established only a few posts along the river system. It was not until the Gold Rush to the Black Hills in 1875 that the Anglo invasion began, and in subsequent years the lands ceded by the Indian tribes were thrown open for settlement from time to time. The land was free, thus inviting the young, the adventurous, and hardy settlers to commit their lives to homesteading in South Dakota. Though many failed despite their sacrifices, population grew and South Dakota was admitted to the Union on November 2, 1889.

One of the young hopefuls who went to South Dakota in 1898 was Grace Fairchild, a Wisconsin woman who had just graduated from the Platteville Normal School with a teachers certificate. Seeking a job teaching school and no doubt excited about starting a career on a new frontier, she went to Parker, South Dakota, where she not only taught school but soon married a widower, Shiloh Fairchild, who had a son as old as she was. Hearing about the new lands open to settlement west of the Missouri, the Fairchilds moved to the short grass country with their two small children in 1902. There in old Stanley County, where the Sioux cession had been opened up to settlement under the Homestead Act, they took a claim of 160 acres. Settlement of that region had begun earlier, but after the extension of the railroad west of Pierre in 1907, settlement increased at a rapid rate. There was a high tide of settlement until the drought and grasshopper year of 1911. Then the tide went out and did not return until the high prices of World War I. The ebb and flow of settlement was always affected by war, drought, and depression.

Through feast and famine, Grace Fairchild stayed on her South Dakota homestead. She raised a family of nine children, kept body and soul together in the lean years, and managed to find a way for all of them to get a better education than most homesteaders' children received. Married to a man who was ill-fitted for the life of a pioneer, she took on increasing responsibilities as the years went by. In 1930, she and her husband separated and divided the land holdings. However, when she left the old homestead after spending a half century there, she had put together 1440 acres of South Dakota land, most of it clustered around the original claim of 1902.

Mrs. Fairchild was an unusual person. She was intelligent, hard working, and motivated by a fierce desire to make a better life for her children. Of the thousands who took up homesteads on the last frontier, it is doubtful if a large percentage had the perseverance, vision, and drive to make a bunch-grass claim grow into a sizable wheat and livestock farm. Many of them lacked the capital, the knowledge of dry farming, and the pioneering qualities of staying power, hard work, and the sacrifice needed to succeed, and pulled out and went back east where they came from or moved on to Montana, Idaho, or the Pacific Northwest where free land was still available. But Grace Fairchild stayed and made a success in a difficult land ninety miles west of Pierre.

In her last years, Grace Fairchild began to bring together her records and pictures, and started writing her recollections. Her daughter, Mildred (Mrs. Mitchell Vesas) kept the material together and in the fall of 1969, the recollections and letters were sent to me.

In my rewriting of these materials, I have frequently rearranged the story, written whole new paragraphs, rounded out incidents, and attempted to say in a more understandable way what Grace Fairchild was trying to tell. But at no time have I caused her to say something that was not said or implied in her original manuscript. She was a woman of forceful character and strong language, and her life story is the history of the last frontier in microcosm.

A word of appreciation is due these associates who helped with the manuscript at one stage or another: Mrs. Mitchell Vesas for answering all the questions about her mother; Dr. Wayne Wolfe for his valuable suggestions in design of the book; Helen B. Wyman, artist and wife, for her drawings; Dora Rohl and Mary Baurichter for typing the manuscript; and Wilbur Sperling for his support of the University Press. Mary Pryzina deserves special thanks for it was she who first called attention to the existence of the Fairchild recollections.

Grace Fairchild and her experiences west of the Missouri stand as an important reminder of the pioneer days that South Dakota celebrates in its Centennial Year, 1989. She personified the experiences, the sacrifices, the grit shown by thousands of early settlers. She would probably be flabbergasted to learn that this book, *Frontier Woman,* first published in 1972, is now in its sixth printing and promises to be a long-lasting reminder of "how it was in the good old days west of the Missouri."

Walker D. Wyman
March 9, 1989

Frontier Woman

The Life of a Woman Homesteader
on the Dakota Frontier

Table of Contents

Page

I .... I Made My Bed............................ 1

II .... "All Out for Pi-erre" 9

III .... Getting Settled on the "Goddamn Claim" 15

IV .... Children and Schools 27

V .... Our Neighbors West of the Missouri........... 37

VI .... Interesting People and Places 53

VII .... Livestock and Rattlesnakes 61

VIII .... Never a Dull Moment..................... 73

IX .... Expanding the Homestead, and Taking Root.... 87

X .... Building a Home and Buying Tractors 95

XI .... Farming the Dry Country 103

CHAPTER I

I Made My Bed

*"You just can't tell the truth
about South Dakota without lying."*

*"I remember one winter when it was so cold that
when I set a tea kettle full of hot water outside, it
froze so fast that the ice in the tea kettle was still
warm."*

Trials of a Wife

In all the years we lived on our South Dakota homestead, I
can't remember when my husband didn't have something ailing
him. He was about as much of a misfit in that short-grass country
as could be found anywhere. He had no trade or savings and little
interest in farming, but when the cattle country west of the Missouri opened up to settlement in 1902, he wanted to go after a
homestead there where the short grass grew, and get rich raising
horses. We went out in 1902, made a home and raised nine children, but Shy, or Shiloh as his parents named him, never quite
fitted into the life of a homesteader. While the family broke the
sod, fought drought and grasshoppers, and made a home, Shy sat

1

in the shade and complained about his aches and pains. When people came into the barnyard to buy some horses, he sprang to life, for horses were the only things that excited him. He would visit with the buyers, show them the good points about the horses, and when they left, would come into the house and say he ached all over. In the early years on the homestead I would rub his back with liniment, and he seemed to feel better. He surely wasn't the kind of a homesteader you read about that opened up the West and built the country with hard work and just plain grit.

One day a young man from the little settlement of Pedro came by and told us that he had some "electric liniment" at home that would cure all aches and pains, and said he would send us some. It looked like we might make a homesteader of Shy after all. When it came, Shy was lying down, complaining of his troubles. I pulled out the cork and started to apply it across his shoulders and back where he had the pain. It must have been pretty powerful for it burnt my calloused palm like sin. I poured an extra big palm full and clapped it on. Some of it ran off his behind and trickled down his front side where it touched some tender spots. He jumped off the bed like a shot from a cannon, hollering "Jesus Christ, I'm on fire," and danced around like a man crazy in the head. I ran for the water barrel, got a pail full, and put out the fire with an old fashioned immersion. I may not have saved his soul but after that he was pretty slow about having me rub his back with liniment.

In the early years on our homestead, I yearned for a little beauty to sweeten the hard life we had to live. I could remember the green grass, the trees and the wild flowers of my childhood days in southern Wisconsin, and longed for something to brighten up our little log house on the dry plains. I planted some flowers and a garden after grubbing out the cactus, and after spreading manure around got some pretty things to grow. One spring I asked Shy to plow a few furrows around the yard so I could set out some trees. He was mad because I wanted him to "fool around" this way doing woman's work, so he plowed up the whole yard. It was years before the native grasses came back and then they came only in spots. Whenever it rained, the mud was carried into the house and when it was dry—and that was most of the time — the dust blew all over. If I had been smart I would have waited until he was away from home and plowed the furrows myself or else got some help to do the job.

It was such things as these that made me wonder many times why Shy could think of taking a wife and family to a country like this. We were ninety miles from Pierre and ninety miles from a doctor when seven of my nine children were born. Homesteading on the dry plains was a hard life even if everybody pulled together.

It was a harder life doing it the way we did it. After many years we divided the property and Shy moved into a shack of his own. Things did not change much, but I could now run the homestead without having a husband always around messing up things. We may have been barefoot and poor, but we somehow lived through it, and saw a better day. I knew that the Lord was with us in the years when snowstorms killed the livestock and grasshoppers stripped the crops and gardens. There wasn't much else favorable. One of our neighbors lost his mind, and his wife kept him busy carrying lignite, or coal, from one side of the basement to another, day after day. But we never had it that bad. I will admit that sometimes in the winter months living on a South Dakota homestead was hard on everybody, but always there was another spring. Even when the cattle bunched up along the fences in the late spring snowstorms, with birds on their backs picking at grubs, there seemed hope for a better year ahead. Yes, I made my bed in 1898 when I got married to Shy Fairchild, and moved to western South Dakota four years later, but when I look around at our 1440 acres, I find the bed a good place to grow old in.

Early Days in Wisconsin

I was born in Soldiers Grove on May 30, 1881, but my father soon moved the little family to a small farm on the banks of the beautiful Wisconsin River. We four girls were allowed to play on the river, wading, going out in the boat, or skating on the ice in the winter. To show us how dangerous the current was, my father tied me to the end of a long pole and pushed me out farther and farther in the current until my feet went out from under me and it turned me upside down pretty fast. When he finally pulled me in I had learned what would happen to me if I went out alone. The river was a mile wide at our place and though we often rowed across it, we were always careful when we went swimming or wading or got into the boat.

The little town of Woodman was just two miles from our farm and since we owned the only skiff on the river, we rowed passengers across and back for 25 cents. Many a blister I have had from the oars, and I always had callouses by the end of the summer. But it was fun, and besides it gave us girls some spending money. My younger sister and I often took a little skillet and some matches and our fish poles and rowed across the river to a lake or bay off the river, and there we could catch sunfish and bass as fast as we could pull them in. When noon came, we built a fire on land, fried our fish, and had a meal fit for a queen even if we were only 7 and 9 years old and farm kids on the Wisconsin river. My Aunt Leona would often let us take her little boy with us. He always

3

obeyed us when we told him to stay back from the slippery banks of the river, so no accident ever happened. We would throw him the little fish and he would string them on a willow stick. My aunt said that she was not afraid to let him go with us as long as Gracie was along. Of course, that made me more careful than ever.

On our side of the river, the farms were not large but there was a lot of timber still standing and ready to fell. My father cut wild hay across the river where a nice prairie ran back from the banks. It didn't take much to carry the haying machinery across the river since he only used a scythe and a big wooden rake until time for stacking. Then he would borrow a wagon, swim the team over with it, then leave it there until he was done. But the horses would swim back and forth each day behind the skiff. My, that was a thrill to hold the reins behind the boat while my father rowed. When we went to visit my mother's folks in Millville, we had to do the same thing, only then the horses had more of a struggle pulling a buggy across the current.

In order to have some ready cash, my father ran a little business besides farming. He bought logs, railroad ties, and hoops for barrels. These were cut from the woods during the winter by the farmers and hauled to the river bank. There they were branded and piled ready for rafting down the Wisconsin to Prairie du Chien where they were sold to a saw mill. How we children loved to play around the logs when they floated along. We would jump from one to another and see how many we could step on and get off of before they rolled over. Of course, father was usually not far away and this made us bolder than we might have been if there alone. We soon learned that if a log began to roll and we couldn't make the next one, we should throw ourselves on our stomachs on one with our toes over one log and our hands touching another, crawl to safety. It was fun because it was dangerous. Now and then, a runaway raft would come down the river and every one was out with log hooks and ropes to catch it. If it should bump into other log rafts, it might tear them to pieces.

We had another sport on the river — hunting turtle eggs. We would row to a sand bar, beach the skiff, and then start searching for trails leading from the water to the sandy banks. The turtle digs a deep hole and lays its eggs, and goes about its business. I've often found a dozen in a hole. The shells are soft and the insides look like a hen's egg. We would dump them in our skillet, along with the sand that seemed to get there, too, and have a feast. All summer long we kept a little jar of fat and some salt in the skiff and were always ready to cook up some turtle eggs, sunfish, or anything else fit to eat.

4

My father rigged up a light with a reflector on the skiff at night and during the high water in the spring we would go to the shallow water to spear fish when they would be spawning. We got a lot of big catfish, buffalo, and suckers. Once I helped a fisherman run a trot line, and he caught a 90 pound catfish. What a fight we had getting it into the boat and keeping it there. All the neighbors had a meal of it.

Living on the river made me love the outdoors. How I longed for a brother instead of a little sister to roam the hills with me. I begged my mother to adopt a boy but she always quieted me by saying that I was tomboy enough to make up for two boys. I guess I was. If I hadn't been a tomboy as a child, I don't know how I could have ever moved to the South Dakota frontier to homestead when I grew up and got married.

I can't remember when I didn't tote a gun and keep the family in squirrel and rabbit meat. First I had a BB gun, then a rifle, then a breech-loading shot gun. My father gave me twenty-five cents for every crow I brought in, and this kept me in ammunition. Maybe I got my shooting eye from my grandpa Wayne. He was an Indian scout and a great hunter, and took great pride in his ability to hit a squirrel in the eye at fifty yards. I was pretty good myself. Once I shot against twelve boys and won a gun, a horse, a cow, and ended with a bawling out from an uncle when I made a poor shot.

I loved horseback riding. My father always kept good horses and wanted me to learn how to ride well. When I was eleven, I won a side-saddle in a 4th of July race, but never used it much even if riding astride and bareback shocked the neighbors. They wondered what would ever happen to the tomboy down the road.

In the fall, we could hardly wait for the ice to get thick enough for skating. We skated on it when it was so rubbery that standing in one place an instant too long would have plunged us into the river. Only once did I ever go through the ice, and then I was lucky enough to sink into an air pocket. Uncle Will, Leah, and I were on an ice sled with the sail catching a strong wind, on our way to Boscobel. Leah was hanging on to the sail, all having great fun, when suddenly our sled broke through and we plunged down into the big air pocket beneath the ice. Luckily, our sail saved us, for it stayed above the break-through. We clawed our way out of the icy water and hurried home. Our clothes were as stiff as boards but we were none the worse for the ducking. Many times after we moved to South Dakota I wished we had enough water to fall into in summer or in winter.

Those were care-free days, with six or seven months in school, a few chores to do, and freedom to roam the hills for berries, nuts, and wild crab apples. What a delicacy, wild crab apples steamed on top of a wood-burning stove and served with cream and sugar.

The hills of southeastern Wisconsin were full of old lead mines dating back to the pioneer days when the early settlers, called badgers, dug holes to find the veins of lead. I used to lie on my stomach and look down into the dark pit, and wish that I could find a way to get down to the bottom and back out again. But I never did. Since they were never marked or fenced, it's a wonder that we didn't fall in and disappear so completely that we would never be found again.

One day when I was wandering through the woods I stepped over a log smack on to a sleeping porcupine. Both of us were pretty surprised but I was up and away with nothing more than a batch of quills in my shoe. One time our dog came home with his nose full of quills and what a time we had getting them out. We had to tie his feet and blindfold him, then pull each one out with pliers. It made him sick, and the rest of us sicker to have to hurt him so much.

Snakes were always beautiful to me. I often went with my uncle in the fall when he hunted for rattlesnake dens on the sunny side of the hills. He sold the fat which was used in medicine and was very expensive. Since I've lived on the dry plains, I've killed many rattlers and boiled out the fat, but never sold any. My husband used it on his stiff joints and for rheumatism but I never saw any improvement in his work around the place.

When I was seven my folks moved to Boscobel in the winter months so that my older sisters could go to high school. We had a cow and my father showed me how to hitch it to a sled in winter and ride around town. We put a rope around her neck to guide her with and when ready to go, we braced ourselves and twisted her tail, and away we went. It was fun for us, but in the eyes of some of the people it seemed scandalous that parents would allow their children to do such things. When we moved back to the farm for the summer, the old cow hauled us around in a little wagon in between milking times.

When spring came I roamed the hills looking for the first May flowers and violets. Later, I picked the yellow May apples and squeezed the juice into my mouth. They were so good when ripe, but such a nasty mess when still green. From these childhood days I learned to love nature and to understand it.

My father worked for the Sherman Nursery Company for sixteen years. He was always bringing flowers, plants, and shrubs home for us to set out. He taught me how to graft and bud trees. To show us the marvels of nature, he once grafted eight different kinds of apples on one tree and topped it with a pear. That was a

6

funny sight to see a Sheepnose apple beside a Russet, a Whitney Crab, and a Monmouth summer apple. Father taught us the names of the trees and shrubs in the catalogues. We would pore over the beautiful pictures and try to make ours bloom like them.

One of my earliest recollections is of playing in my grandfather's boat. This he used to haul freight on the Mississippi River and the Wisconsin. When the Wisconsin-Fox Canal was dug, all the big boats on the Wisconsin River quit running and smaller craft took over the business. Grandfather beached his big boat in a little inlet and we children would run up the ladder and play on the deck, making believe that we were grandfather and his crew fighting Confederates and pirates. We knew the story about his experiences in the Civil War, about his boat loaded with potatoes on the way to New Orleans being waylaid, the potatoes seized by the Confederates and the boat turned loose. It made him so mad to come home empty that he and his four brothers joined the Union Army although they were far too old for fighting. Though they came through without a scratch, they must have felt better after having helped defeat the Confederates for stealing grandpa's potatoes. From all the stories in the family, I believe my Scotch-Irish grandfather must have been a pretty rough character. He drank too much and loved to gamble, but he did bring his earnings from the boat home to my thrifty Dutch grandmother, and she put it into land and livestock and managed to educate their children. All in all, I think I would have enjoyed knowing him and I wish that I might have made a trip to New Orleans with him.

Moving to South Dakota

Looking back on my Wisconsin childhood, I can think only of the pleasant things. There must have been some hardships since we lived through depressions as well as good times, and always close to the land. But I did get to high school and then to the Platteville Normal where I took the two year course to become a rural teacher. Hearing that teachers were in demand in South Dakota, I went out there in 1898 and got a job at Parker in the southeastern part of the state. I taught only a year before getting married to Shy Fairchild, a widower who had a son as old as I was. There was much talk about the land west of the Missouri River opening up for settlement. This had belonged to the Sioux until they ceded it to the government and took smaller reservations. Both Shy and his son, Fred, wanted to go get some of this free land. All I could do with two babies was to go along. Looking back now on this crazy

7

idea of moving into the dry plains part of South Dakota for the sake of free land, I think of the poem by Benet that goes like this:

> *I took my wife out of a pretty house*
> *I took my wife out of a pretty place*
> *I stripped my wife of comfortable things*
> *I drove my wife to wander with the wind.*

My husband and Fred went ahead to build a house and I was to follow later in the spring. It was arranged that Shy would meet me in Fort Pierre where the railroad ended, and we would go from there to the new home ninety miles west, near the present town of Philip. Some have always followed the will-o-the-wisp, some to a better life for themselves. Others have found only a place where they wore themselves out so their children could have a better chance. I only knew that my husband wanted to seek our fortune on that new frontier. So I packed up and without looking behind, boarded the Northwestern Railroad for Pierre, April 6, 1902. For better or for worse, I had made my bed.

MY SOUTH DAKOTA HOME

Thomas Tolton

God took a ray of sunshine,
Mixed in a bit of dew,
And made the dearest place on earth,
Where skies are ever blue.

He made the rolling prairies,
The hills and valleys, too.
In this little bit of heaven
Where friends are ever true.

Then he hung a starry lantern
Up in the midnight sky,
To guide the wandering stranger
Who might be passing by.

And no matter where I wander,
Though the whole world I may roam,
In my heart I shall remember
My South Dakota home.

Pioneers of the Open Range/ Haakan County South Dakota (Pioneer Club of South Dakota, Midland, South Dakota, 1965), p. 128.

CHAPTER II

"All Out for Pi-erre"

"The coyotes are so poor in Dakota
they have to lean against their shadows to howl."

"Pi-erre, Pi-erre, every one out at Pi-erre. This is the end of the road," sang the conductor. The train stopped and folks started out. It was 2:20 on the morning of April 7, 1902. I gathered up my six-months baby, Leah, and two-year old, Emma, and moved out with the rest.

As we left the coach we were hit by a cold wind, filled with sleet and snow. I glanced around the platform for my husband, but he was not in sight. I hurried into the station. It was warm inside and I put the little girls on seats and looked around. I thought maybe Shy had over-slept and would be there any time. The depot cleared and we were the only ones left. I decided that as long as the little girls were comfortable I would just stay in the waiting room until morning.

About an hour later the station agent came in. He asked me, "Where are you going? I have to close up and won't open up until 8:00 in the morning." I explained the situation and he told me how to get to the Lock Hotel which was quite some distance from the depot. I gathered up the girls, wrapped them in my cape, and

9

went out. I found the hotel where we registered, and were given a nice warm room. I put the children to bed but Emma was very fretful and I didn't get much rest. I was almost out of money. I had just two dollars left and the world looked pretty bleak as I tried to sleep that night.

The next morning I decided to go to the First National Bank and identify myself to Mr. Branch. I told him I was stranded and needed money, and that I thought my husband had an account there. He told me he had and gave me five dollars and quite a lot of advice as to how and where to leave word in case Shy would arrive and miss me; also where to go after I got to Ft. Pierre which was across the river.

Staying in Pierre

By then it was time for the ferry to Ft. Pierre so I got the babies and luggage. I had to make two trips to the landing, first with the luggage and then with the children. We had to wait in the cold until they loaded up for the trip across the Missouri. Emma was cross and feverish. On the other side a wagon, drawn by four horses, hauled us to Ft. Pierre about a mile and a half away.

There were two hotels in town. As I did not know which one to go to I went where the driver stopped first. I got a room and put the girls to bed and began to inquire around to see if I could find my husband. No one had seen him in town.

By evening Emma was very sick so I called the doctor. He said in his opinion she had measles and pneumonia. Not having had any experience I was at a loss as to what to do for her. The doctor left medicine. My mother had always used cold packs for a cold so I used them. We had no more than got settled for the night when the bed bugs began to march, whole armies of them it seemed to me. I stayed up all night trying to keep them off the babies. Before morning the room was splattered with blood streaks where I had killed them. When the doctor came the next morning to see Emma I asked if there was another place with less bugs, and if I could move Emma. He said I might try the other hotel, so he wrapped her up and carried her to this other place for me. For his kindness, he probably picked up some well-fed bedbugs as well as his $1.00 fee.

An elderly woman, Mrs. Oldfield, ran the hotel. It was clean and warm and I think she saved Emma's life. She put a flaxseed poultice on her back, an onion poultice on her chest, and a hot-water bag at her feet and kept at it until the measles broke out. Her fever went down some but the pneumonia ran its ten-day course.

We were in Ft. Pierre a week before Shy came in to get us. He had forgotten the date when he was to meet me and had not got the mail for ten days. When he did get my letter he started out. It was the 15th of April when he arrived in town and it was snowing. It stormed for two nights and two days. It had been a hard winter on the prairies. Snow had been on the ground since December 1. The cattle were poor. This storm was sure to take a lot of them.

On the Way

After staying in Ft. Pierre eight days we started out for the claim, following the road to the Black Hills used by wagons and stage coaches. The mud was so thick and sticky that it looked like black glue and stuck to everything. Shy had come in on the running gears of the wagon and was taking out lumber for the house. He had bought bows and canvas and made a covered wagon. Then he loaded the wagon with twelve-foot boards, leaving a space in the middle for the girls and me. The groceries and feed were stowed in front and behind, but the load was not well-balanced and was too heavy for the team of black mares. They had stood in the livery barn all week in town so were soft to begin such a trip.

When we left Ft. Pierre, we had to cross a draw that was deep and narrow. As the wagon went into the hole the front end of the lumber hit the bank ahead and shoved the load almost off the wagon. Then the lumber hit the bank at our rear and shoved the load almost on to the horses and threw us against the bows that held up the cover. The babies were banged up, and I got a badly bumped nose. The lumber had to be reloaded. We made five miles this first day and the mares played out. We were not prepared to stay out on the prairie all night so Shy rode back to town and got a team and buggy to come get us, and take us back to Ft. Pierre for the night. The next morning we started out early in the borrowed buggy which we were to leave and another person was to return it to the owner.

When we came to the bad crossing again I was braced to take the bump. I had Emma at my feet and Leah in my arms. As we went into the hole the front wheels hit the bank and Leah left my arms as if she were greased, landing among the horses' back feet in front of me. At Shy's "Whoa!" they stood still and I reached down and pulled her in unhurt. We made it to a homesteader's shack that evening — ten miles.

In this country the air is clear and the prairie and the sky met miles ahead and they seemed to be moving as we drove along. Although cramped on a load of lumber I could see the rolling plains rising and falling into depressions, disappearing ahead against the sky. On this great prairie Scotty Philips had miles of high woven-wire fence enclosing a big herd of buffalo. We were fortunate to see several large herds of them. I was told he had five hundred head in that one pasture.

Scotty Philips had married an Indian woman and ran a big cattle outfit. He had a nice home up the river from Ft. Pierre, but his squaw preferred her tepee. They had several children. It was said that Scotty offered any eligible white man 500 head of white-faced cattle as his daughter's dowry.

The next day we made about twelve miles and stopped at another homesteader's place. The woman there had been bitten by a rattler. Her husband had slashed the wound and sucked out the poison and then given her whiskey. She had been in a drunken stupor for three days, and he planned to keep her so for a couple of days more. We had to get supper and look out for ourselves. The roof of the house was covered with sod, and the floor was dirt. The snow had melted and run down the walls, and the floor was muddy. Shy had planned on having a sod roof for our house but I knew then I would hold out for something better.

My doubts about homesteading increased as we rode along this trail. The storm that had kept us in Ft. Pierre eight days had caused a great deal of damage for the stockmen. It had been a long hard winter, so I was told, and stock was poor. All the way out I saw dead animals, bloated with their feet in the air, or being washed down gullies. I realized what a calamity this was, and I wondered what I was getting into. My husband was worried over the loss of so many horses. I was able to pick a few spring flowers when we stopped to let the horses eat and my spirits rose somewhat.

It was raining the next evening when we got to Hayes forty-five miles west of Ft. Pierre. Mr. Hopkins, the storekeeper, had us come in for shelter even though his sister and a hired man were recovering from small-pox. Shy and I had been vaccinated, but the girls had not. However, since there was no other place to stay, we bedded down there.

The next day as we crossed Willow Creek we got stuck in the mud. Just as Shy was unhitching the team to let them feed while he unloaded, Dan Bierwagon came along with a four-horse team. So Shy hitched up again and Dan put his four horses on ahead. Still they could not budge the load. Dan said that a freighting outfit from Pedro should be along in a little while. "They have six-horses and I am sure they can get you out." In about an hour they did come along and pulled us out. Because of this delay we got caught between stopping places and when we made camp we had to take the canvas off the wagon and use it to cover us during the night. We kept the children warm but we did not sleep much ourselves.

The next station was at a sheep ranch. We were not so sure we wanted to stop because the freighters that pulled us out of the mud told us the owner of the place had been picked up and put in jail for murder. A boy who had been herding sheep for this fellow got suspicious when he saw blood in a wagon box as another hired man had disappeared shortly before. The young herder had left his sheep and had taken off across country on foot keeping to the low lands as much as possible and hurrying as fast as he could, never stopping to talk to anyone until he was east of the Missouri River. He reported his suspicions to the authorities and they got in touch with the Stanley County sheriff. An investigation was made and they caught the man, Kunnecke, disposing of a body in a brush pile. He was arrested and was later convicted of killing six men. His wife, or the woman he lived with soon sold their holdings and we never heard of her again. His reasons for killing was to keep from paying wages to his hired men, but he also killed some of them and robbed them. They found the horse one man was riding but never traced its rider. This is the story we had heard, so we were uneasy that night.

We had followed the old Deadwood Trail most of the way, until the road branched off to the northwest at Ottumwa. The evening of the seventh day we pulled into John Griffins place, ten miles from our claim and here we spent the night.

The next morning we started on the last lap of our journey. It seemed to me that these final miles were endless. The prairie was like the ocean with great swells and troughs, and at the top the sky and ground seemed to meet. But when we reached the crest the horizon had receded beyond the next wave, and on and on and on.

The sack of grain on which I sat got harder and harder but there I had to stay in order to keep the girls contented. When they slept I would sit up front with Shy or walk beside the wagon. I could not do this for long though, because my shoes would pack full of mud, too heavy to carry. The mud clung like tar to the leather.

Occasionally we would see a coyote loping ahead of us, and there were always dead animals along our way. I had been warned about rattlesnakes but we didn't see any on the way out. Frequently I questioned in my own mind how a sane man could be dragging his family into such a desolate country. The sod shacks and log houses along the trail looked dismal, and I wondered if the women who lived in them had any happiness. Here we were leaving settlements with frame houses, churches and good farm land going into a desolate unknown. Funny though it never occurred to me to act like a balky horse and refuse to go any farther.

There was plenty of land just as good or better than that on which Shy had filed and it would have been so much nearer to town and to other people. I remember, hearing a neighbor ask Shy "What are you going to that goddam country for anyway?" and he

13

answered "To get away from people." Well, he was doing it in a big way. He was doing what he wanted to do, "and to hell with anybody else."

After eight days in the wagon, on May 4, 1902, about sundown, we got to the Fred Fairchild place. He was married to Eleanor Stobbs who had filed on a "relinquishment," which was a claim not yet proved up by the first settler. The original settler had built a little log cabin, and here we stayed with Eleanor and Fred for nearly a month while our house was being roofed and finished, sleeping on the dirt floor. Our claim was a mile and a half east. This is how I began my life as a homesteader ninety miles west of Pierre. I was not to go back to that town for three and a half years.

CHAPTER III

Getting Settled
on the "Goddamn Claim"

There is "a difference of opinion regarding South
Dakota climate. Some claim it is nine months of
winter, three months of wind, and the rest summer.
Others maintain that it is nine months winter and
three months late in the fall . . . ."

A. B. Gilfillan, *Sheep* (University of Minnesota Press,
Minneapolis, Minnesota, 1957), pp. 83-88.

Building a House

I might have known that Shy wouldn't have a house ready for
us to live in. Fred and his wife and a hired man had come out in
the fall of 1901, and after getting settled in the little twelve by
fourteen foot homesteader's cabin that someone else had built,
they were to get out the logs for our house. There wasn't much
timber in that country except along the rivers. Just seven miles
away was a creek and there they found enough logs to build our
house. But the winter set in early and the heavy snow made it hard
to move them up to our claim, even if the men were young and
full of vinegar. When Shy got out there in March, little had been
done. He hired Bill Lyle, an old hand at dressing logs, to work on

15

what had been dragged over to the place. Each log had to be smoothed on two sides so it would lie close to the next one. The three men, with the help of my step-brother, Harry Schadt, soon had a log house laid up that was fourteen by twenty-eight feet square, and nine feet high. Most of the houses were made either of logs or sod and covered with dirt. A homesteader had to build with what he had on hand. I didn't want to fight dirt all my life, having it drop into the food on the table, or have the roof fall in when it rained, so I insisted on a loft and shingles on the roof. But we had only enough logs to make it seven and a half feet high unless we left the west end open. So we took the logs and added them on top, made a garret or loft, then boarded up the end with twelve inch lumber and covered it with tar paper. This kept out the wind but not the cold, but it was all we had for a year.

Learning how to live in a log house even with shingles and a loft took a lot of changing around. I hadn't wanted to go west of the Missouri in the first place, but now that I had made my bed, I wanted to make it as comfortable as I could. It is never good to cry over spilled milk, but that would have been very easy for me. I knew that when Shy sold out his place and livestock in Parker he had $1700 more than the mortgage, and that was plenty of money to get settled on our claim out West. That was enough to build a nice frame house of lumber shipped out on the railroad to Pierre from Minnesota and Wisconsin. As it was, we spent $1,000 building a log house and a few out-buildings. This was silly but that is the way Shy wanted it.

Our house needed repair all the time. Chinks between the logs opened up letting in South Dakota daylight and that was pretty cold at times and pretty hot at others. We banked the house with manure in the fall and this helped keep it warm in the wintertime. When the smell got bad in the spring, we knew it was time to take the insulation away. The barn, the hen house, and the hog house were dug into the hillside and roofed with poles and hay, all pretty nice in dry weather but mighty nasty in wet weather. In time we had a buggy shed, sixteen by twenty-four feet, made of lumber. It was the only dry building on the place, and so it was used for a shop and granary, too. Shy was more interested in keeping his horses and their gear dry and warm than in keeping his family out of the wind and sun. When he spent the money we had set aside for the roof for the house on things for the horses, I was fit to be tied. The price of a $100 saddle would cover a lot of roof with shingles, and shingles would make a better top for the family than a saddle would make a bottom for him.

Adding a Room

The next summer I talked Shy into buying lumber at Pedro to build an extra room on the west side of the house. We each drove a team hitched to the running gears of a wagon, and with the children settled down in a box fastened on my wagon, we went to Pedro on the Pierre-Black Hills trail. It was a thirty mile trip one way but we made it in a long day. The next day we loaded up and started home. We expected to stay at Frank Rood's road ranch but found the place locked up and the Roods gone. We looked around and found an old mattress in the shed, so with what we had, we made out all right for the night. There was enough food for the children the next morning, but not for us, so we headed for home as hungry as bears. We had a very steep hill to climb to get out of the breaks surrounding Pedro. My team made out all right but as we came up the hill I wondered every minute when something was going to break and let us roll off into the deep gullies on each side of the trail.

Shy had the best team and so had loaded heavier than I did, but his horses couldn't make it up the grade. I had to unhitch and put my team ahead of Shy's and the four horses brought his load up to the top in no time. Since the lumber was going to make another room twelve by fourteen on our house, I never minded doing a man's work, even some of the cussing needed to haul lumber over thirty miles of ruts and dust.

The next time we saw Frank Rood we told him that we had used his shed for a bunkhouse but were pretty hungry before we got home. He said, "Well, for goodness' sakes, I thought everyone knew how to get into the house. All you do is crawl through the wood box on the side of the kitchen. The only reason we lock up is that my wife has quite a bit of silverware which she thinks ought to be protected from people who don't live around in this country." Since they lived next to the Sioux Indian Reservation and were on the main stagecoach drag between Pierre and the Black Hills, they did have a lot of strangers through there who might be short on silverware.

Chimney Troubles

We got the extra room added that summer, but the stove was always a problem. The stove pipe ran up through the roof and there was nothing around it to keep the shingles away from the stovepipe. As I cooked I looked up so much that I got a crick in my neck. After the house got on fire the third time, Shy decided we should have a chimney made of rocks, but the only place he could find to put it was in the middle of the house and roof. The stone mason said the chimney could be built off on one side of the room but Shy insisted that we have it in the middle and almost directly in front of the stairs leading to the attic. This stove and chimney took care of heating and cooking, but its location surely made it awkward for me in the kitchen. It didn't bother the children much when they were little and I managed to get around it, but every time Shy went upstairs he bumped into it. He was so mad that he moved our bed down to the main room. One day when I went from the kitchen to the main living room, I forgot to look for little feet when I squeezed by the stove, and stepped on a toe, popping the nail right off. I was furious because my kitchen and cookstove were so poorly placed and I never let Shy forget about it. Whenever anything turned up like popping a toe nail, or when I turned on him, Shy would grab his coat and head for the barn in a hurry. Later one of the hired men said, "Whenever I see Mr. Fairchild coming out of the house on the run, I know there's been hell to pay inside."

Our house, part logs and part frame, was airy and nice in the warm months. In the winter, the logs would shrink and the chinking of mud and manure would fall away, leaving cracks big enough for a good blast of snow and freezing cold just off Moosejaw to come through. Many a time we got up in the morning to find the floor covered with snow. Onetime a traveler who had stayed in the loft said, "I don't know how to get downstairs." One of the boys said, "Just follow my tracks."

Shy was No Pioneer

Many years later we covered the logs with paper and siding and lined the kitchen walls with wall board. This was done over Shy's objection. He always said that as soon as he had made a stack of money he was going to get out of the country, so didn't want to waste any money dinging up our place. Fifty years later I am still living in the same log house, but have added a few improvements over the years. Shy went to his reward in 1940, at the age of 85, still hoping to make his fortune and head for some new frontier.

My husband was never intended to live on the plains where hard work was needed to make dreams come true. I have wondered many times why I ever followed him to South Dakota but then, I loved him. He had never learned to read until we were married. His first wife had read to him from her church magazines but after we were married, he had to learn to read the hard way because I would not read to him out loud.

Shy was bothered by some of the ideas talked about in these early years. Our country was growing up, new counties (including Stanley county) were being set up, and taxes were needed to

18

support them. He hated a man who used his brain to make a living and he heartily damned the people who wore white collars and worked for the government. Anything new that I might read about, as new crops or livestock—except horses—was shrugged off by him saying "Something one of those white-collared fellers thought up." But he was always ready to listen to information about breeding or racing horses.

Salt-rising Bread

In the early years on our homestead, I was busy trying to make my husband happy and I tried to do everything that he wanted me to do. After awhile it seemed that he was trying me out to see how far he could mold me to his liking. He seemed to want to take me back twenty years or more. One time he asked me if I had ever heard of salt-rising bread. I remembered an old lady who had made it, but all I could remember about it was the awful smell. He wanted me to try and make some. I couldn't find a recipe or anybody who knew how to make it. But he kept asking for salt-rising bread and finally I said, "Well, if you will tell me how I'll try." About all he could remember was that it was made with salt, water, and flour. I knew enough about fermentation to know that it would have to be kept warm. I mixed up a batch of dough and covered it with blankets, and from time to time I peeked underneath to see what was happening. For four days it stayed just the way it was when I started it. After a few more days I decided to throw it out. What it did to the gophers or prairie dogs, I never did find out. Years later I found a recipe in a farm paper for salt-rising bread and made a batch for Shy and the family. None of us liked it even if it did turn out a light loaf with a sour smell. I never heard any more from Shy wanting salt-rising bread.

Gun-powder Tea

One of Shy's other demands was to get some gun-powder tea. I finally got hold of some from Sears Roebuck. When you live ninety miles from a town, a Montgomery Ward or Sears Roebuck catalogue gets read more than the Bible or Shakespeare. When I saw gun-powder tea listed, I ordered a pound and made some tea. I suppose that I did not brew it the right way or his taste might have changed. Anyway, he did not like it and said that it was because the mail order houses were using a substitute for the real stuff.

With or without gun-powder tea and salt-rising bread, life with Shy got harder each year. When my father and mother came to see us, they stayed just a day or two then headed back to Iowa where they had moved. My sisters visited us one at a time and they always encouraged me. Heaven knows they didn't want me traip-

Frontier Woman

sing back with my children for them to look after. If I hadn't been
tied down with the babies coming every year, I might have got a
job teaching. But why dream about the impossible? I was settled
down on a South Dakota homestead, one that was best suited for
livestock and certain crops, and having made my bed I had to lie in
it. If there was never enough hay to carry us through the winter,
or enough pasture for the summer, I had to face up to the problem
and find an answer. We always had more horses than cows, and
they took most of the grass and fought the cattle away from the
haystacks in the winter. This went on for years until 1917 when
we got rid of a lot of horses and paid off the mortgage for the first
time, and for a few days were free of debt. What a wonderful relief
after years with this burden hanging over us!

Corned Beef

Once when my sister Leona visited us in the spring we were
short of meat and on a homestead when you are short of meat you
are short of food. The chickens were too young to eat and it was
too late in the spring to butcher a calf. But Shy said that he knew
how to corn beef. He corned it all right and it spoiled. That fall we
butchered a hog. Leo Hagler was working for us and he said "I'll
show you how to cure the meat and I guarantee it won't spoil."
We had a whiskey barrel that we had got for a water barrel, and we
used it to put the meat in. Leo put in about two inches of salt,
then a layer of meat, a layer of salt, a layer of meat, until all the
meat was covered with salt. Then he made a brine strong enough
to hold up an egg and covered the meat with about eight inches of
that. Well, it was cured all right. It was cured so well that it
petrified. But we used it even if it was hard to chew.

Sweet Corn in Salt Brine

A thrifty German neighbor, Mrs. Stuffenberg, later showed me
how to cure meat right. It took time to learn to do all these things.
The first sweet corn I ever put up was in salt brine. Before using it,
I had to soak it for hours in several waters, and in the end added
sugar and plenty of cream to make it go down better. I doubt if
there were any vitamins left, but at that time we worried more
about filling stomachs than about proper diet. When I canned
corn, I boiled it twenty minutes, put a tablespoon of salt on top of
each quart jar, fit on a rubber, and screwed down a glass-lined
metal lid. That would come out as sweet and good as any I ever
tasted. Of course, tomatoes and cucumbers were easily kept in
jars. As I look back now, I realize that life would have been hard if
we hadn't had salt to keep things with, or if we hadn't been able

20

to get out on the prairie and get jackrabbits when we were short on meat.

Sauerkraut in a Whiskey Keg

Another neighbor, Mrs. Tony Motch, taught me how to make sauerkraut in a whiskey keg. While it was working and was pretty smelly, we put it on the porch. It was not unusual to see the kids take out a handful as they passed by. They just lifted up the lid and helped themselves with a wooden fork left in the barrel for their use. In the winter we chopped out the sauerkraut with an ax.

After we got our place going, we had plenty to eat—butter, cream, eggs, chickens, meat, and garden vegetables. Once when Ed Runhold sat down to dinner with us he looked over the table and said: "All I can see that come from the store is coffee, sugar, salt, and pepper." He was right. We had some cash coming in all the time to use for food and clothes and necessities for the ranch. Now and then we sold some steers and horses, but the bank took all that money to pay the interest and what was due on the mortgage. We milked a few cows and sold the butter. We had some chickens and sold eggs and old hens in the fall. For several years the mail carrier stopped at our place to change horses, and this gave us a few dollars. There were always some people from the East out looking for South Dakota land, and though we were crowded we fed them and bedded them down, and this brought in some cash.

Keeping Boarders and Roomers

One time when Shy was away, a couple of land agents drove in about dark and asked if we could put up sixteen people for the night. Of course, I told them we would keep them since there was no place else for them to sleep except on the prairie. I fed them, got their beds ready around the floor, and then went to the barn where I had four cows to milk. I picked up my milk pail which I had set off the table on to the floor and someone had used it for a spittoon. I was so tired, far into one of my pregnancies, and was so mad I could have killed the whole bunch. By the time I got my pail cleaned, the kitchen was pretty well cleared out, and by the time I got in from milking everyone was in bed. Not one had offered to help me milk. I've a sneaking feeling that they thought a hell-cat was loose and they better stay under cover. With my own family, I bedded down twenty-three that night. But it was a hard way to make a little cash on the side.

Late one night Felix Byrnes and Frances O'Connor rode in, hollered that they wanted to stay all night with us. We were in bed, but Shy got up and helped them put their horses in the barn and brought them in. They were pretty well soused. I doubt if they even knew their own names. I told Shy to put them in the attic and he showed them the way up, and told them to look out and not hit their heads on the roof. The next morning I heard a thump and some swearing. Frances had hit his head. That woke Felix up and he went to get up and tipped over the sanitary cot and threw Frances out on top of him. They looked pretty sheepish when they come down stairs.

We were doing all right in these early years. Within three years we had put together a herd of seventy-nine cattle and a bunch of horses, had several acres of prairie broke and planted, and were about free of debt. I had a family to look after, and more and more of the running of the ranch fell upon me. I suppose I did neglect Shy in these years and not give him the love that he needed, but I was so busy raising a family and a homestead that I had little time to be just a wife. We just drifted apart.

Shy Buys Longhorns

I always held my breath when a horse trader came on to the place, for that meant Shy might make some big trade that would put us in debt for something we did not need. One day when a horse trader came by, I guessed the worst would happen, since I did not have any respect for him and knew he was a sharp dealer. He wanted Shy to go with him to look at some cattle. I was satisfied with what we had and was real happy that we were getting along so well. Knowing both Shy and the horse trader, I was a little afraid of what this "going to look for cattle, might run into. Shy had mentioned earlier that we should have more cattle, so I got him to promise that he wouldn't buy any until a good chance come along. When they left that morning, I thought that he wouldn't do any buying that day, but would come home and think about it awhile before he acted. When they did not come back for three days, I was ready for anything, debts and all. They had by-passed the cattle they had planned to see west of our place and had ridden 110 miles to Rapid City where Shy had been talked into buying ninety-one head of cattle from Corb Morse. So they came home with fifty two-year-old steers, forty cows, and a bull, all Texas stock with long horns, big heads, and little bodies, a sorry looking sight to me. We had enough hay for our herd but not for this hungry bunch.

Before winter came, we rounded up enough hay to carry the whole herd through if we had mild weather. While this was being hauled in, we built a hay-covered shelter to give some protection to these Texas longhorns. As luck would have it, winter came early and stayed with us until April 1 before we had much of a break. The cows ate their heads off, the hay dwindled to nothing, and the ones carrying calves got weaker and weaker. This new stock had, of course, been bought on time, and our old herd had been mortgaged for security. To look after them we had to hire a man. By spring the hay we bought to keep the longhorns alive cost us $10 a ton. That debt of $4,000 seemed as big as a million to me as I looked across the prairies and saw cow after cow go down in the snow. We would tail them up and move them to the haystacks or open country, and scatter them as widely as we could. When they walked into a waterhole up to their bellies they were too weak to get out by themselves. Shy and Ed Stephenson rode day after day trying to save them, but while they were dragging one out of a waterhole another would be drowning somewhere else. By the time the grass was up enough to keep an animal alive, we had lost twenty-six head of cows and six steers. We ran the rest of them on grass all summer and sold off the steers that fall. The money was turned over to the bank but it didn't make much of a dent in the debt. This longhorn fiasco convinced me that if we were to make our goddamn claim into a ranch, I had to take charge of the whole thing.

Blizzards and Debts

Blizzards were forever with us in a South Dakota winter, and everyone of them killed off some livestock. During one storm we had a cow step into a waterhole, get one back leg wet and then it froze. The next spring her leg dropped off. She was a nice cow and Shy didn't see why he couldn't make a wooden leg for her and so he did. It looked as though it might work. When the ropes were untied, the old cow got up, back-end first, then on to her front feet, then she looked around, gave a big bawl, kicked both hind legs, and the wooden leg flew through the air and hit Shy in the face. He made up his mind right there that the old cow could walk on three legs the rest of her life as far as he was concerned. That fall we fattened her awhile and butchered her. We couldn't tell any difference between a three-legged cow and a four-legged one when the steaks were on the table.

The blizzard of May, 1905, was the worst in that country in many years and it caused a good many ranchers to go broke. It began with a rain on May 2 and the grass greened everywhere. Most of the ranchers had turned their livestock out of the barnyards and corrals. Shy and the hired man had gone to Pedro to get some posts. I had done a big washing and had it hung on the line.

Frontier Woman

The first cold rain began to fall when I was bringing in my clothes, and it kept on raining for two days and two nights. The first evening of the storm a peddler drove in and wanted a place to stay. The two men who were building our fence moved in with their bed rolls. It looked as if it might be right cozy in our little house until the storm was over.

When the rain turned to snow on the second day, we knew we were in for it. For two nights and a day, the snow piled high. The waterholes had been filled by the rain and the snow made them so slushy that when cows walked into them, they couldn't get out. The cattle began to drift on the second day and one by one they froze to death or drowned in the waterholes. We found some of ours forty miles southeast of our place, and herds from the Cheyenne drifted down to our claim. Hundreds of head died in that storm. We lost ninety-one of our 168 head of cattle. Many ranchers had made the mistake that Shy had made by buying Texas Longhorns that had never lived through a South Dakota winter. Since they had mortgaged their livestock for security, they turned what was left over to the bank and went through bankruptcy. Shy and the trader, Lum Elshire, were the only ranchers around who carried their loan on through and paid off their debt. It took us fourteen years to pay ours off, with interest at ten per cent and one year we paid twelve percent compounded semi-annually. Everything we made from livestock was turned over to the bank. These were the years when I learned to garden and raise chickens, enough to keep the family fed. I sewed for the children, and even made them some shoes. Between Shy's lack of sense and the snowstorm of 1905, we nearly lost our goddamn claim.

The Ft. Pierre-Black Hills Trail

Our claim was on the stage road half-way between Ft. Pierre on the Missouri and Rapid City in the Black Hills. Along the trail about every thirty miles there was a road ranch and postoffice where the stage drivers changed horses. One of these postoffices was at our place. The freighters followed the Deadwood Trail which was shorter than the mail route. We kept a string of six or eight horses for the stage drivers, and also bedded the passengers down and fed them when they got there at night. I have often cooked for as many as twenty-three drivers, freighters, and land-seekers and found beds for them in our two-room log cabin. This gave me contact with the outside world and though the life was hard, I enjoyed talking to everybody who brought news from outside. Besides, it was a source of cash. I charged twenty-five cents for meals and the same for a bed, whether it was on the floor or on a cot. Pedro, thirty miles north, was on the Ft. Pierre-Black

Hills freighters trail, so we could buy everything from lumber to chewing tobacco or "Electric liniment" there. These trails and travelers kept the door open for us to the big world beyond. When the Northwestern Railroad came through Philip in 1907, we felt that a new day was at hand. No more freighting our groceries and feed from Ft. Pierre. It had taken me three and a half years to get back to Ft. Pierre after I left there with Shy on the wagon in 1902. The rails now connected me with everything I knew before I went West—my sisters, my parents, and store goods—and some of the lonesomeness began to go away.

Shy and Grace Fairchild

Feeding the geese

Fun on the Fairchild ranch

CHAPTER IV

Children and Schools

"It's hard to tell the folks back east about homesteading in South Dakota. Things are just too darn pretty out here."

The Old Stone Churn

One of my proud possessions in the early years on our claim was a stone churn with a dasher. I made enough butter to keep the family going, and as I churned I could think about what had to be done next. When the butter had come the children liked to dip out a cup of buttermilk all flecked with gold. It was as special as bread just out of the oven with wild plum jam.

One day one of the children broke the old churn, and I asked Shy to get me a new one when he went to town. I wanted a "Daisy" churn, which was a glass jar with a dasher like an egg-beater. I might have known that he would botch the job. When he came home he had a fifteen gallon affair, big enough to churn all our milk as well as just the cream. How I hated that thing! It was so heavy I could hardly move it, and it had to be kept in the hole beneath the floor to keep it from drying out. Besides that, the dam top was a task to put on. If it wasn't on just right, the clamp would slip and off it would come. I used it for years and every

27

time I used it, I cussed Shy. After a good many years, we used it to treat wheat before sowing, and I was never able to wash the poison chemical out of it. I sure was glad when it fell to pieces and I could burn it. But in its day I churned hundreds of pounds of butter and the children drank hundreds of gallons of buttermilk out of it. Goodness, what I didn't put up with in these early years and how I hated a lot of the things that made life hard.

Having Children: The First Six

When I got mad, I could always get some comfort out of thinking about the children. I had two babies when we went to our claim in 1902, and in the next few years, I had seven more, all born at home. A tenth child was too premature to count. We didn't read about over-population but we helped bring it about.

The first two children, Emma and Leah, were born at Parker with the help of a doctor and Jane West (Reimer) who showed me how to take care of babies. I was then eighteen years old and as ignorant of the facts of life as a girl could be, not much beyond believing that babies were found under gooseberry bushes.

Jasper was the first child born on the claim. A few days before he was born, Scotty Ferguson came along and wanted Shy to go with him to look for some horses. Nothing could stop my husband when some one mentioned horses. I didn't want him to go away because I would be alone with the hired man and anything could happen. But he went anyway, saying that he would be home by evening. When night came, there was no Shy. I kept supper hot on the stove until 10 o'clock. The little tots and the hired man had gone to bed early, as usual. As I sat by the coal-oil lamp, crocheting, until 2 o'clock in the morning, I worried about what might have happened. I had all of the next day to worry since Shy and Scotty never rode in until dark. They drove in ahead of them a string of ten Indian ponies. Shy said he had paid cash for his, but Scotty had just laid claim to some loose ones on the prairie. Later the Indians came and took all but one which they allowed Shy to keep.

When Shy and Scotty were bringing these ponies home, they had stopped at an old woman's claim where they put the ponies in her corral and spent the night in her cabin. She had only one bed in her little place, but all three slept in it. While there Shy hired her to come over and take care of me when the baby came. I was pretty upset about it. He knew full well that I had arranged with Mrs. Griffin who lived eight miles away at the Top Bar ranch, to come when we went after her.

28

The old woman came over the next day. She was filthy and smelled to high heaven. She opened her suitcase and it was filled with dirty clothes. She said she didn't have any water on her claim so couldn't do any washing. A lot of homesteaders didn't have any water in the early years, but hauled it in barrels from a spring or little creek or from a neighbor who had dug a well. That evening Shy and I had a little talk. I decided that I had to let him know who was having the baby and that I wouldn't let the old woman touch me or my baby. The next morning we put her on the stage for Pedro and somehow she got back home.

A year and a half after Jasper came, Joe was born. It was a hard winter and the snow was deep. Shy wouldn't go after the woman I wanted to help me, so we had to get Mrs. Kurtzman who lived not far away on a claim. I got up on the third day and carried on as usual. Fifteen months later, Clinton arrived and Mrs. Anderson, another neighbor, came over to help a few days. Byron came along fifteen months later, with the help of Annie Michaels and Dr. Verley who did a little doctoring while he homesteaded twelve miles east of our place.

To have six children in less than eight years is something of a record. You would have thought I was in a race to see how fast we could get that new country settled. I decided it was time to call a halt, and in the next four years I didn't have a child. Once during those four years I thought "Oh, my God, I am pregnant again" and took a heaping table spoonful of quinine and went to bed. Pretty soon I began to feel queer. I staggered around the house trying to get my breath, and wondered if my last day had come. After walking around for a couple of hours, I decided that after this I'd better quit bucking nature so I could be around to look after the family we already had.

Having Children: The Last Three

When Wayne come along, we hoped to have Dr. Verley come over to help again. It was the year of the drought in 1911 and I was home alone with the children. Shy had taken our cattle to the Sand Hills of Nebraska where the grass was a little better. By this time we had a barbed-wire telephone in the country and so I called a neighbor and had one of them go after Doc Verley. It began to snow and got real bad, so I called and had the neighbors tell him to turn back. I hitched up the team to go after Mrs. Stuffenberg, but when I was ready to go, I wasn't sure I could make it, and I was afraid I might have the baby in the buggy. So I stayed home and sent one of the children for a bachelor homesteader, Louis Johnson, and had him drive over to get Mrs. Stuffenberg. They started out but when they were only ten rods from the house, the horse balked. So he had to unhitch and go back to his own place, round up a team, and drive over to the Stuffenbergs again through two miles of rolling country in a storm after dark. Mrs. Stuffenberg made it to our house an hour before the new baby came.

To have a baby in a snowstorm after a dry summer was not the best time to have one. The chinking between the logs had shrunk away leaving big cracks. The strong wind drove the snow through the openings and by morning my bed was covered with snow. Mrs. Stuffenberg took a tubful off the covers but the baby was as snug as a bug in a rug beside me. We kept each other warm even if the inside of the cabin looked like the great outdoors.

While Shy was in the Sand Hills, I had a team of horses to use when I needed them. Two cows freshened in the fall and had to be milked twice a day. We had two sows and they farrowed that fall, having eleven pigs apiece. Between nursing the baby and looking after the other children I had more than enough to do. But the two old sows made all sorts of trouble for me. Shy had watered a few rows of corn all summer long to make some fodder, and this is where the old sows went every time they got out of the pen. I chased big pigs and little pigs all fall, carrying on like the U.S. Mail through snow and hail and sleet.

Wayne's birth made five boys and two girls. I wondered if I was ever going to stop having boys. Eighteen months later I had my answer when Mildred was born. She was our pride and joy. The other children were old enough to enjoy her and she had such a happy disposition that all she had to do was let out a yip and someone would pick her up. Even when Russell came along a year and a half later, Mildred was still the little charmer. Russell weighed only four pounds, so we had to favor him a lot until he got started Doc Verley managed to get there in time to help with both Mildred and Russell.

If I had known anything about birth control I would have taken advantage of it. But now as I look back on our family of fine, healthy, normal children I am glad that I didn't know much about it. During these years when there was no doctor around in our whole country, I gathered all the medical information that I could lay my hands on. I read doctors' books and articles on how to care for children, and talked to anybody who could tell me what to do when a baby came. I didn't know anything about vitamins, but we did have plenty of vegetables in the summer and I stored plenty in the root cellar for the winter. Our own fresh eggs and meat, butter and buttermilk, and plenty of milk and clabber seemed to be all that was needed to keep kids in good health.

Starting a School

When it was time for Emma to go to school, there wasn't any available in that part of the country. I wrote to the county superintendent in Ft. Pierre, ninety miles away, and asked him how we could get a school started. He told me that one member of the school board, William Griffith, lived at Leslie, thirty miles from our place. If Griffith was satisfied that there would be enough children to fill a school, one could be started. The settlers had to furnish the school house and the desks, stove, and books. We would have to find a teacher, but the school board would pay the wages.

This was all that we needed to know. We knew that we had enough children. The Fergusens living eight miles away had two children. The Hankins and the Anderson families each had one. With our two children and Catherine McKeen, we had a total of seven to start with. In time, the Fairchild family alone would keep a school going even if every other homesteader moved back East.

Fred Fairchild gave up his claim and so we bought the twelve by twenty-four log house for a school. It was partitioned into two rooms. Mrs. Hankins lived too far away for her children to walk to school every day so she brought a stove and some housekeeping articles and lived in the one room with her children. We furnished the other room with a little sheet-iron stove and a blackboard. Shy made some benches and a table, and school began. Carrie McKean, our first teacher was a lovely girl. She was just seventeen, had finished the eighth grade back East, and the county superintendent gave her a permit to teach. When we got school under way, the superintendent came out to visit it and he approved all that had been done. The children seemed to be learning. Just having a school available made life look a lot better to me.

While walking back and forth to school — a mile each way — our little girls found many interesting things along the road. As the sun sank earlier and earlier, I warned them to come home early and not linger along the way. But one night it began to get dark and they had not yet come home. I thought I would scare the little tykes and teach them a lesson. I threw a buffalo robe over my shoulders and went out to meet them. When I could hear them chattering, I got down on my hands and knees and began to growl and carry on. But I had forgotten the collie dog that went to school with them and he came running up to me wagging his tail and making over me. The children had no fears about a big bad wolf that growled like their mother and smelled like a friend to their dog.

31

At the end of the first year, we decided to take the school down and rebuild it on our land near the home place. This would save us the trouble of transporting the children during bad weather, or sending them off wrapped in a blanket and tied down at the stirrups on their horse, led by the hired man. But locating a school close to our house was a mistake. That fall a lot of homesteaders came out to that country to take up land and when school opened we had eighteen little Americans hungering for learning — and playing Blind Man's Buff. We had hoped that Carrie would teach the school another year but she wanted to go on to high school. Bert Dibble, a homesteader who lived five miles across country, took the school that year. This was just what the school needed. Some of the boys were getting to be hard to handle and a man teacher could do the job. He was as stern as they come and believed that old saying about "spare the rod and spoil the child."

We went over to Leslie where the Indian school run by the missionaries had been closed and got some desks and other equipment and with these our log cabin school really began to look like a school on the inside. Dibble could not teach the second year because he was homesteading and had crops that had to be attended to. We looked around and found Ellen Hanrahan who started the year. She had a permit to teach until she took the examinations over all the subjects taught in the school. When she didn't pass, Bert Dibble came back to finish out her term.

The next year Jasper started to school and Maude Kitterman was the teacher. She taught it for two years, and by this time the school had twenty-nine pupils. Families were moving in to take up claims faster than the teacher supply increased. That little log house was filled to the rafters and the only teachers we could get were homesteaders' wives or daughters, and very few had ever taught school before. Sometimes the blind led the blind. If I hadn't had to care for a family and do a lot of ranch work, I would have taken over the job of teaching even if my brood made up a sizeable part of the school.

Having a house next to a school with twenty-nine pupils is not exactly the best place to live in South Dakota. When a storm would come up, I had to take care of the whole bunch sometimes, and always I had to look after those who lived a long way across the prairies. I fed and bedded down a good many children and I still have to get my first thank you from the homesteaders. When the settlers got together and organized their own school district, I sure enough didn't cry my eyes out. A new school was built a quarter of a mile away. Over the years we had some good teachers and some bad ones, but through it all our children made their grades and liked to go to school. The taxpayers had a running fight about the location of the building. It was moved three times, each time closer to the center of the district. But as far as we were concerned, it made no difference for our children had horses to ride. Goodness knows the Fairchilds always had horses running out of their ears. Some of the settlers had nothing more than a team of plow horses.

Education After Grade School

What to do with the children after they had finished the little rural school was a problem. We wanted them to go on to high school so they could go out and hold down a good job. I didn't want them to settle down in that wilderness west of the Missouri and have to fight as hard as we had to make a living. Looking around, it seemed that the homesteaders who made good had good educations — the Haxby, Morrisons, Davisons, and others. But to send a big family through high school seemed impossible. There just wasn't enough butter and egg money to pay their board and room.

Emma was the first one ready for high school and even if we didn't have the money, she was determined to go anyway. She worked for her board and room for four years and showed the other children that it could be done. Besides, she learned how to keep house and how to get along with the people she worked for. During the flu epidemic in 1917, when Dr. Gearhart fell and broke his hand, she drove his car for him. She had never driven a car before but wasn't afraid to try it, and managed it very well. Philip High School was closed because of the epidemic so she didn't miss anything working for the doctor day and night. He paid her $5 a day. This was big money and helped her buy clothes and get the other things she needed to pay her way.

After finishing high school, Emma was at loss to know what to do. She was of a mind to go on to college but didn't have the money, so decided that a short business course might be a stepping stone. She had a catalogue from the Mankato, Minnesota, Business College, and that looked like the place to go even if the fees were high. I signed the note at the bank with her, got her the money, and away she went. She studied there four months and got a job at the Hormel Packing Company. Later, she got a civil service job at South Dakota State College in Brookings, and managed to take classes at the same time, finishing her Bachelor's degree in 1924.

One year when Emma was at Brookings, she thought I was getting into a penny-pinching rut, so she wanted me to get away from home and come to Brookings and take some courses. I agreed to go. She rented a house and all of us — Jasper, Joe, Clint, Mildred, and Russell along with Emma and me, lived there for six months. I did most of the cooking but still had time on my hands so I took a course in applied arts and one in government. While five of us were going to college, Byron and Wayne were home with Shy running the old homestead.

When the boys came along to high school age, we decided to have them take the short course at South Dakota State College. This was a six months season for farm boys and took them away from home only in the winter months. This seemed the best place for them to go. Jasper, Joe, and Clint took the short course for four years, but Joe and Clint did take one year of high school first. Byron went to Pullman, Washington, where he stayed with my sister while he went to high school, then he went to the University of Washington for a semester or two. Wayne wouldn't go to high school or take the short course, but spent his school years having a good time and working around the country wherever he could get a job. Maybe he did learn farming by seeing how others did it.

Joe was the farmer and he loved everything about the farm. When he was at South Dakota State, he liked the creamery course better than any other. When he came home he was anxious to put into practice some of the things he had learned but it wasn't always possible to do everything. He wanted some pure-blood cattle and so Shy bought four head and gave one to each of the boys. When they were gone six months of the year taking the short courses, I had to keep the records for them. Their studies helped us build a good herd of cows.

Mildred came of school age in the depression of the 1930's. She spent each year in a different high school, not because she just wanted to move around, but because she had to have a board and room job in order to go to school. A consolidated high school had been built in Marietta Township only seven miles away and she went there for the first year. Her second year was spent at Jasper, Minnesota, and her third year was at Proviso Township High School, Maywood, Illinois, where her sister Emma, now married, was living. Mildred finished her senior year at Philip High School, then went to South Dakota State for four years and later she had two more years at Iowa State College at Ames.

When I look back now and see how the children managed to get an education, I feel very proud. It wasn't easy to start a school in a big country where the settlers were so scattered and had so little, and it wasn't easy for the settlers' children to ride horses so far to school. Not many of the children went on to high school in the early days in South Dakota. All but one of ours got some education beyond the grades. All of them had to make their own way by working for board and room, and this did something for them, too, even if it was hard at the time. They had learned to work at home and they were willing to work to get an education.

HOT AND DRY WEATHER SAYINGS

"It was so dry the water had only 50% humidity."

"It got so dry that the cattle starved down so they could crawl through the holes in the chicken wire and then hide among the chickens, which was annoying."

"If a drop of water hit a man, they had to throw a bucket of dirt in his face to bring him to."

"It's so dry in South Dakota the buzzards have to fly backwards and wear goggles to keep the dust out of their eyes."

"One day I saw a coyote chasing a rabbit and it was so hot, they were both walking."

"They say you are a tenderfoot until you can taste the difference between the dust of Texas, Kansas, and Dakota."

CHAPTER V

Our Neighbors West of the Missouri

> When Jim Braddock saw Jim Griggs bring in a new-
> born calf in zero weather and put it in the barn, he
> said: "You're the first damn rancher I've seen who
> knew enough to save a calf. Most ranchers don't
> know enough to pour water out of a boot even if
> there are directions on the heel."

Opening the Indian Country

That part of South Dakota where we lived had been Sioux
Indian territory until a few years before we moved there in 1902.
It was good grass land. The cattlemen and sheepmen had discovered it around 1880. They had built their log houses and corrals along the Cheyenne and Bad rivers and the little streams running into them, and their cattle and sheep roamed all over the
country. Some of them paid rents to run their stock on Indian
land. When the Indians ceded the land below the Cheyenne to the
government, it became public domain, and was open to settlement
under the Homestead Act. Hundreds of people took up claims
west of the Missouri, and we were among them. After the railroad
pushed west from the Missouri in 1907, thousands of people came
out to file their claims, many not expecting to stay longer than the
eight months needed to get title so they could sell it.

Frontier Woman

The Homestead Act allowed only the husband or wife, not both, to title. A woman could file a claim, then get married, and the husband could file a claim for himself, and in that way they could double the size of the ranch. But a woman could not file on a claim after she married. It always looked to me as if the government was run by men and all the laws were made for them. So women had to take up claims before they got married. Some of them came out to take up a claim after their husbands died.

My mother was one of these widowed homesteaders. She settled on a piece of land next to ours. Her little cabin was across the creek and on the hill where she could look across to our place. We had an understanding that if she needed help she would hang a piece of black cloth on her door. One time she was sick for two days and we didn't see the black rag. She lived there just long enough to prove up and then we bought her claim.

Indians

In our early years, most of our "neighbors" lived ninety miles east of us, beyond Ft. Pierre, or on the Indian reservation twelve miles south of us as the crow flies. There were a few small ranchers settled along the rivers, and a few of them had started farming. We had some neighbors we called "squaw men" who had married Indian women. Dan Powell was one of them. His wife was well liked by everybody, and respected, too. Kid Rich was another squaw man. But the best known of all the squaw men was Scotty Philip who had come out to the Black Hills after gold and stayed to marry an Indian girl and become a rancher. Most of our squaw men had got hold of a good piece of Indian land for their cattle by marrying into the tribe.

The old Indian trail between the Cheyenne River Reservation north of our place and the Rosebud and Pine Ridge reservations south of us ran past our claim. The Indians often camped on our little creek and came over to swap things with us. I liked their bead work and buffalo berries and they liked some of our garden stuff. They always acted friendly. One of them gave me quite a start one time when I didn't know that anyone was around. I was at the sewing machine with my back to the door. Something told me to look around. There in the door stood the biggest squaw I had ever seen. She wasn't fat, just big and tall. She nearly filled the doorway. Wearing moccasins and walking lightly as most Indians do, she had come inside the door without making a sound. All she wanted was to do some trading. The Indians never lingered long, but we did have some visits with them. I was hungry to have somebody to talk to. Besides, I wanted to know more about how

38

they lived. Some of the young and even a few of the middle-aged Indians could speak English. They had learned this from the traders, or at the mission schools. But it was hard to get them to do much talking. I loved the little papooses that hung from their mother's backs. They were strapped to a board and wrapped in a shawl, and peered out at the world with their bright black eyes, black hair, and serious faces. I always felt I had a lot in common with the Indian mothers even if we lived on different sides of the fence.

The Poor People Move in: the Wares

As I look back now, most of the people who came out to South Dakota had little of the world's goods but hoped to get ahead by hard work and good luck. One of these settlers was Will Ware who moved out to our country from Indiana with his wife and eight children. They didn't have much money and not much more sense. We let them move into the little school house up the creek until they could fix up something to live in. Will was one of the slowest moving people I have ever seen, as slow as molasses in January, and so he never made much headway. Shy sold him the little fourteen by fourteen lean-to on the school house for $12 and let him work around our place cleaning our barn and doing chores to earn the money. Of course, a man with eight children and no money would have three hound dogs. That first year they must have lived mostly on jack-rabbits and the oatmeal they had brought along. In the winter, ten of them along with the hounds lived in the lean-to and a little tent which they staked out and banked with dirt to keep out the cold. Now and then he got a day's work with some of the settlers, but the family had a hard life.

One of the Ware boys, Harry, had stayed in Pierre when they drove their wagon through there on the way out. He had a job working in a hotel. When Shy was in Pierre in the fall, he brought the boy out to work for us. He paid him $20 a month, and this helped the Ware family keep going. When Harry settled down with us I was in bed with a new baby. One morning I discovered a little animal crawling around on my bed sheet. I called Anna Bellany, who was working for me when I had my baby, to come look at it. "Look here," I have never seen anything like this before." "Why, that is a louse," she said, "I've seen 'em hundreds of times." I was frantic. I had lived with flies and mosquitoes, but not with lice, although I had heard about them all my life. We looked in Harry's bed and it was fairly crawling. Then we looked in the children's caps and sure enough they were full of lice. One of the boys had been sleeping with Harry, and his clothes were covered with the little bugs. The funny part of it was that we hadn't noticed the children scratching.

There was just one thing to do, boil everything. Anna put on a boiler of water and poured in some carbolic acid and boiled all the clothes. Then she sprinkled the bed clothes and mattress with the acid and must have either killed every louse around or shriveled him up so he would never do any more biting. We sent Harry home to get different clothes. He put on a pair of clean overalls over his old pants, and so he got loused up again right away. We went through the whole thing again, sent him home, only to have him come back with his clothes still crawling. I told Shy it was time to get rid of the boy or we would never get rid of the lice. When he had been home on his de-lousing trips, he had scattered these Ft. Pierre hotel lice all over the Ware family, and in a fourteen by fourteen house they spread pretty fast. They didn't have enough clothes to change into so they could boil them and clean up. So they stayed lousy until spring. That family of ten and their three dogs looked more like a bunch of mangy calves than human beings on the homestead frontier.

Settlers weren't always clean and they didn't have many clothes, but they were too proud to get the reputation of being lousy, even if they could take the scratching. The Wares didn't seem to care about either.

That fall we had more potatoes than we needed so we told Will Ware that if he wanted to dig them he could have half. He said he would be glad to get some good old potatoes again. He brought his team over, hitched on to the plow, and started down the rows. The Ware children were there to pick up the potatoes. But we noticed that he didn't plow up many and I knew that something was wrong. When I dug out a few hills with my hands, I saw that he was leaving half of them in the ground. This man was so slow-moving and easy-going that he couldn't even plow up a row of potatoes. So we stopped him right there and plowed out the spuds ourselves, but we did offer him some of them. We put them in our cellar and told them they could come get what they needed any time they wanted to. After awhile, I discovered that something was going wrong. When I sent the kids down to the cellar after potatoes, all they would bring up was little ones. Come to find out the Wares were taking all the big potatoes and leaving us the little ones. This seemed to be the attitude of some other homesteaders when we went out of our way to help them get started on their claim. The South Dakota frontier wasn't any place for the weak ones.

Cogills

The Cogills settled north of our place and we also had some problems with them. They didn't belong out west of the Missouri. One time they were out of chicken feed and asked us if we could lend them some corn. They sent their brother-in-law, Betz, down for the feed. We told him where to find it in the barn and to take a sack of corn out of a bin there. When we looked in the bin the next day our seed corn was all gone from the barrel, but the other corn was there. He had taken the biggest and best ears we had saved for seed. I suppose he thought the best was none too good for their chickens.

In the spring, the Cogills came down to our place with one horse hitched to the tongue of a wagon. They said the other horse had died of starvation over the winter, and wanted to know if they could borrow another from us so they could drive to Philip for supplies. But Shy wouldn't let them have one since they misused their animals, and so they went on their way driving the one horse. I was really peeved about this because we had plenty and if one had died on the way to Philip, it wouldn't have made any difference. Shy always liked horses and had more than he knew what to do with, but he would never help a man who mistreated them.

Breemes

John Breemes, his wife, and their five children settled on a homestead one mile east of us, and when they got there in the fall, they had only $40 in cash to build a house and live through the winter. This family had been born in Holland, had got over to New York somehow and then a few years later had migrated to Spink County, South Dakota, which was some 100 miles east of the Missouri. When they heard about the Indian lands being open to homesteaders, they pulled stakes and headed west to get free land. They settled on their 160 acres, built a little log shack, and not having any lumber for a door, they hung a canvas over the opening. The first winter was pretty hard going for them, but somehow they lived off of the country. Since we had more potatoes than we needed and some beef, we sold them some, mostly on time. They were devout Methodists and tried to live up to their religion. But people who are hungry are apt to do things they wouldn't do if their bellies were full. Outside of being such religious fanatics, they were pretty good neighbors.

During the drought of 1911, grass was very short and our cattle pushed the fence down and got out. Mr. Breemes had set out a little grove which he was very proud of. Of course our cattle hit for this grove where they ate the leaves, pulled off the little limbs, and really pruned the orchard. The Breemes had taken the

41

cattle up to their house and held them for damages. We paid the $5 which they asked, and knew that the money would be well spent by them for food. Not long after that, Breemes went to North Dakota to work in the harvest fields, leaving the family without much of anything to live on. Our cattle got out of the pasture again, and the calves headed for the Breemes' orchard where they did some more pruning. Mrs. Breemes and the children had quite a time getting the calves penned up at their place, but they did get a few of them, and then came on over to our place to ask for damages. I liked Mrs. Breemes and it hurt me to hear her say that they were out of food and didn't have any money to buy any. So I said to her, "We will go over to Marietta where there is a little store and get you what you need, but don't go to the trouble of trying to shut up our cattle again. Just let us know if they get into your orchard."

Since the Breemes lived only a mile away, their kids and ours played together a lot, although theirs were older than ours. One day Fred and Dave came over to play with our young boys. Pretty soon Jasper came up to the house with his hands pretty nasty, and I asked, "What is the matter?" He said, "One of the boys dug a hole in the ground and did his BM there, and told me there was something in there for me if I would dig it out."

Another time, these kids were picking apples up the creek and they got into my garden and busted up a few melons that were not very plentiful that summer. I told Mrs. Breemes that she had better keep her kids out of my garden if she wanted them to live, meaning that I had sprayed the melons and it might poison boys as well as bugs. She couldn't believe that her boys would hurt anything in my garden! Charlie Sears, who was working for us that fall, stopped at the garden one day and took a muskmelon out and ate it. He got very sick. He told Mrs. Breemes, "For God's sake, keep your kids out of that garden. That old hellion has poisoned the melons!"

Sichtermans

On the south of our claim were the Sichtermans. I remember when Mrs. Sichterman was Jane White living with her brother on a homestead not far away. Garrett Sichterman had filed on a claim joining us. Before they were married, she bought a relinquishment of 160 acres or incompleted claim for $500. When they were married, they moved his shack over on her land so she could prove up on the relinquishment. When she got title to the land, they moved the house back to his place and she sold her quarter section. Garrett mortgaged his land and built a house and a little barn. The children came along every year or so. He got some of the prairie plowed and planted to crops, and earned some money by working for the neighbors and on the county roads. But they were very poor for a good many years. Mrs. Sichterman was often alone and when she got lonesome she would come over to our house for a visit. I made one mistake. I sold her my baby buggy.

We turned our milk cows out at night so they could fill up on grass. Every so often one of them would come up already milked. Back in Wisconsin, farmers used to believe that when cows came in dry from the pasture, snakes had milked them, but we suspected it was done by a two-legged one. One morning when Shy was out after the cows he found Garrett sitting under one, milking her as fast as he could. He looked up at Shy and said, "I was just getting a little milk for the kids. I won't take it all." We felt sorry for the kids and that summer gave them a cow to milk. Since they didn't have a corral or a fenced-in barnyard, and had to keep her on a picket rope, we also furnished some grain for her so she would give plenty of milk. Jane wanted to go to the fair that fall so they turned the old cow out in a big pasture. She went dry and so they were out of milk again. We didn't offer to replace her or to deliver milk to the door. But after that our cows didn't come up dry any more.

Shelton

Another homesteader by the name of Shelton sometimes milked our cows when they got up to his end of the big pasture. Shy had a long cedar post which he used to stake out fence lines, sighting from one to another so the shorter posts could be in line. One day the long post down at Shelton's line came up missing. We wondered where in the world it could have gone to. One time when we were over at Shelton's, we found the answer. There it was, a beam supporting the roof of his little log house.

Mrs. Stuffenberg, a Spiritualist

Old Lady Stuffenberg lived on a claim at the southwest corner of our land. She had been born in Germany, but had come over here several years before. Though raised a Catholic, she had drifted away from the church and seemed to be something of a spiritualist. One day when I was visiting her about three years before World War I, she said that war was coming. She made chills run up and down my back when she told of things that were going to happen. Some of them did happen, too. I really liked to visit with her because she was an intelligent person. There was surely an interesting bunch of neighbors on the homestead frontier. Perhaps we appreciated them because we had so few and little in the way of entertainment.

Frontier Woman

Mrs. Stuffenberg always planted her garden according to the signs of the moon and always had a good one. So I learned to plant my beans in the light of the moon and the potatoes in the dark of the moon, and somehow it seemed to work for me, too. She made beer from an old German recipe that tasted pretty good, but I never tried to make any myself. She taught us how to make blood sausage and how to get the intestines ready for stuffing. She turned the intestines inside out, washed them, and scraped off the inner lining. The she put them in a tub of water and washed them on a wash board just the way she washed clothes. The intestines were then turned right side out again and washed once more. Now they were ready for stuffing. She attached one to her stuffing machine and after filling it with sausage, pushed the lever down and filled the casing. This was repeated again and again until she had all the intestines filled with good meat seasoned with various spices. Somehow she had put together a smoke house and smoked all her meat. Nothing but the squeal was lost when Old Lady Stuffenberg butchered a hog.

Catholic Church is Built

Mrs. Stuffenberg was Catholic, and so were the Motches, Klasses, Harts, Pfeiffers, Hobbes, Gittings, and Gebbes, all neighbors, and most of them had moved out from Missouri to get a free piece of land in South Dakota. They missed their church very much. As soon as they got settled on their homesteads, they build a little church two and a half miles north of us. A priest was sent out and they had an active congregation for a number of years. But when the Catholic homesteaders failed and moved back East or went on to Montana or other places to take up land, the church stood there alone. It was not torn down until 1949. We missed it for it had been a landmark for many years.

Durstons from England

One time an agent brought out a bunch of land-seekers looking around for homesteads. One of the people was Gilbert Durston, who had come from England and how he ever got to South Dakota I don't know. He took a claim right close to ours, and when he had been there a couple of years, he sent for his folks. They sold their holdings in England and with that money they came to America. In the family were his father and mother, both going blind; one blind boy, Curtis; another brother, Herb, his wife and two children. The old man filed on a piece of land joining Gilbert, but there was only eighty acres left for Herb to file on. Never having owned much land in England, they felt that they were regular landlords. Gilbert married Emily Winkler who lived with her parents on a homestead not far away. The Durstons had more land than anything else, and had trouble making a living on it. Most settlers were poor and had it hard for a few years, but these people had it harder than most of them. One winter they had to have help just to keep from starving.

Herb had been a gardener in England but this didn't fit him very well for farming on the dry prairies. In 1912, he was one who got seed wheat that had creeping jenny in it, and the land that he had worked so hard getting ready for crops produced a jungle of this weed that choked most of the wheat. His eighty acres would not carry enough stock to make him a living even after he had a team and a few head of cattle, so he worked out among the neighbors. When he worked for us, it always seemed that the day we needed him most he didn't show up. After this happened a few times, we quit hiring him. We did offer him a job digging potatoes on the share one fall, but he left a good part of the potatoes in the ground. The snow came early, drifted over the potatoes and stayed there all winter. The next spring when we plowed this piece of ground, we turned up potatoes that were as nice as the others had been in the fall. Herb was a better gardener than a farmer.

Mrs. Herb Durstan had been a lady's maid in England and knew very little about house work, as she found it here, and nothing about sewing. One year when the children started school, I made her and the little girls thirteen dresses. The kids had stayed out of school quite a lot of the year before because they didn't have enough clothes. While I was sewing for her she was supposed to come help me so she could learn how to do it herself. When she finally got down to my place it was time to get dinner, so she would get the meal and do up the dishes. Then it was time for her start home since she had to walk two miles, carry the baby, and help the other two or three little ones along. I didn't mind this very much, but she wasn't any help and she didn't learn much about sewing. She was good company and her children behaved, and I liked to have her come anyway.

When Herb was working for us, our oldest, Emma, was learning to cook. One day when I was away, she thought she would make a dessert. She made a custard pudding and flavored it with vanilla. She did not know that the label on the vanilla bottle had been scratched off and another one made with a pencil. That evening the family noticed something strange tasting about the custard, but no one wanted to hurt Emma's feelings by saying anything about it. Herb even ate two dishes of it. About 9 o'clock, he went home for the night. When I got home, I tasted the pudding and knew that something was wrong with it. It didn't take me long to find out that instead of vanilla flavoring, Emma had put in some carbolic acid. Immediately the household was in an uproar. Someone said we should get on a horse right away and ride over to Durstons and tell Herb that he was poisoned. "Suppose he should die, who would be to blame?" someone asked. "If we tell him he's been poisoned, what could we do about it?" We were pretty scared. When Herb came to work the next morning, feeling "much better", he said, we felt much better too, more than he ever knew.

One day, Freddy, Herb's oldest boy, came running down to our place so excited and out of wind that he could hardly talk, but he did manage to say that "Mamma wants you quick." I jumped on a horse and got up there as fast as I could, but it was too late. The baby had come. Mrs. Durston said she just gave one grunt and the baby was there. I looked at it and saw that it was alive and squawking, so I covered it up and started getting things organized around the house. Mrs. Durston had been milking barefooted when she felt the birth pangs and had gone to the house and jumped into bed with her feet covered with cow manure. Looking around I couldn't see much sign of soap and water or that there were any clothes ready for the baby. When Herb brought Mrs. Leverton into the house and said that she would stay a few days, I was glad to get out. I went home, got a bar of castile soap, some baby oil, boric acid, and some left-over baby clothes, and took them back to Mrs. Durston. By that time Mrs. Leverton had washed the baby with a bar of yellow soap. We put my things on the baby, put boric acid in its eyes, and tucked it away. That strong soap caused the baby to have sore eyes for a long time. This was my first experience as a mid-wife. I would rather act as a mid-wife to cows and pigs.

The Durston's blind boy, Curtis, finally got a dog that led him around so he could walk to the neighbors and back. One day the dog led him through a mud hole. When he got to our house he was wet and muddy and disgusted with the dog. He thought the blind was leading the blind. Later he got the dog trained so it would lead him while he was on horseback. He learned to play the accordian and sometimes played for dances in the settlers' homes.

When old Lady Durston died, the old man, Curtis, and Herb's daughter, Emily, moved to Philip and built a popcorn stand. Herb left the claim and moved to town with the family, and worked around town by the day. When his wife died, he moved to Rapid City where he later died. His dream of being a landed gentleman like those in England never came true. A lot of homesteaders west of the Missouri never found the pot of gold at the end of the rainbow.

Hildebrand

When we settled on our claim in 1902, there was a bachelor named Hildebrand who had a sheep camp a mile and half east of us. He lived in a dugout which had been scooped from the side of a hill and roofed over with poles covered with sod. Life in a dugout was about as sorry a situation as a human could endure. It was snug in the winter, but when it rained, the water ran into the dugout and the floor was a mud puddle. His bed was a pile of straw in one corner which he shared with his dog. He cooked on a broken-down stove, his only utensils being a skillet and a couple of pans. He spent his days out with his sheep. If a person stopped to pass the time of day with him, about all he got out of him was a "fine day" or a "bad day" and that ended the visit. He couldn't talk much English and in spite of his name may have been a Mexican or even a Basque brought over from Spain to herd sheep. But he was a homesteader and when the settlers began to move in, fencing the range needed for his sheep, he sold out his land and the corrals to Frank Kurtzman. The homesteaders fenced in their crop land to keep livestock out, and this ended the day when a sheepman could let his sheep run free on the big government pasture.

Kurtzmans

The Peter Kurtzmans lived four miles down creek from our place. He had been born in Luxemburg and she had come from France. They had just moved into their log cabin with their seven boys and a girl the year we moved to our claim, but had lived in a dugout before building their log house. How they all lived in that little hole in the ground is a puzzle to me. But they seemed to be a happy family even if life was hard. The boys missed out on school for a few years and even after we got the school going, the parents didn't keep the boys in school for the six-month term. They had a bunch of sheep and the boys were needed to herd them. I remember hearing them tell once about killing sixty rattlers in the two months they were out with the herd. After awhile, around 1906-07, the Kurtzmans got enough ahead to add to their log cabin and to put in a stock of groceries. Later on, they built another addition, a storey and a half, to the house, and for the first time could sleep the family without stacking them up like cordwood. The place was then big enough to hold dances in, and we had some good times there where we met all our neighbors and heard all the news.

The Kurtzmans were friendly folks and everybody liked them. Mrs. Kurtzman came over to help me when Jasper was born. I had

47

spoken to a woman who lived thirty-five miles away near Powell, and told her that the baby was due on February 10. She could come anytime after February 1. Although Shy had a hired man to help him do his work, he found an excuse day after day not to go after this woman. On February 9, a blizzard moved in on the country. For three days snow fell until the prairie was blanketed belly-deep on a horse. Of course, it was impossible to go after the mid-wife through the deep snow. When I began to labor on February 12, Shy began to squirm, for he didn't want to have to deliver a new baby. Who could he get to take care of me? Since Mrs. Kurtzman was closest to us, he sent one of the boys after her. It took a day to make the four miles and back in the snow, but when he got home, he had Mrs. Kurtzman with him. The baby was born early the next morning and Mrs. Kurtzman had to work with only a little coal-oil lamp for light. When she tied the navel and went to cut the cord, she made the mistake and cut it between the knot and the abdomen of the baby. When the blood began to flow she was nearly out of her wits before she knew what had happened. I held the navel until she made a re-tie. No wonder she decided to go home the next afternoon to take care of her own big family. Mrs. Morrison then came over for a day to help out, and on the third day I took over everything from changing diapers to cooking meals again. The life of a homesteader mother would have been a lot harder if we hadn't been willing to help each other out, especially when the children came and we were all alone. Most men are not much good when babies come.

Morrisons

The E. A. Morrisons were living up at the head of the creek a mile and a half from our place when we settled west of the Missouri. Edward, or E. A. as we called him, had grown up in New Hampshire and then moved out to Iowa with his parents, but not before his father had ducked him in the Atlantic Ocean lest he forget where he was born. The family next moved to Vermillion when that part of South Dakota was being settled. E. A. married Jennie Miner whose folks had homesteaded where Vermillion now stands, and who had proved up a claim near Sioux Falls. Jennie's father was chaplain of the regiment stationed at Fort Randall. Her mother once heard that the Indians were on the warpath, so she gathered the family, loaded them in a wagon, and drove to Sioux City where she got a boat and rode down river to the fort for protection.

The Morrisons moved on to the new state of Washington for three years, and then came back to DeSmet, South Dakota, where they bought a flour mill. When the mill burnt down, E. A. was

48

ready for a new adventure. He heard of the range country west of the Missouri being opened to homesteaders, and decided to head out there. He gathered together 250 head of cattle and 150 horses, and with three neighbors started west. They had a cook wagon and bed rolls, and while the men looked after the stock, E. A. looked for a piece of land that had water and a lot of open country around. He found what he thought he wanted about four miles east of us but Peter Kurtzman had laid claim to the waterhole E. A. wanted and so he decided to look somewhere else. Farther up the creek he came on to the corrals, sheds, and shack of four bachelors who had squatted there and were trying to make a go of it. E. A. asked them if they would sell their holdings and what would they want for everything. The four bachelors talked it over and decided to sell, but said they wouldn't take less than $300 for their shack and corrals and all. E. A. paid them before they could change their minds. Later he told me that he would have given them $1,000 without batting an eye if they had asked for it.

Morrison's nephew filed on the bachelors' claim and this was E. A.'s home ranch for many years. He was a good rancher and didn't believe in having all his eggs in one basket. The Clements brothers south of him had sheep and seemed to be doing pretty well, so he sold some of his cattle and bought a bunch of sheep.

It was around this time that the squatters began to get worried about the settlers coming in, building shacks along the streams, plowing up the prairie to raise crops, and fencing their homesteads. So they began to file their claims, too. In between our place and the Morrisons the Linsay brothers filed their claims. As the story goes, the Linsays had got into the cattle business too fast and had branded a bunch of Texas longhorns that belonged to an outfit that Charles Shannon kept an eye on. When the owners spotted these longhorns with the Linsay brand on them, they sent a delegation of three to have a little talk with them. The cattlemen advised the Linsays to ride far and fast and only hit the high places. When Shy and his son, Fred, came on to the scene in 1901-02, Mrs. Linsay was still on the claim but was trying to sell the livestock and the improvements. Fred bought them, and Eleanor Stobbs, his intended wife, filed on the land. Later we bought the land from Fred since it joined ours. We never heard from the Linsays again.

E. A. kept his sheep a couple of years, then put 1,000 head out on shares with Fred Fairchild. Fred had filed on a piece of land on Spotted Bear Creek, north of us seven miles. It was a good country for sheep. About this time, Fred got the Socialist bug and spent most of his time studying socialism in the shade rather than herding sheep and helping with the lambing and keeping the coyotes

49

away. Of course, he lost sheep right and left and when E. A. finally took the bunch back, he didn't have much more than the seed. The next year he bought 1600 head and had Fred herd them on his range, and this year the sheep did better. Fred either quit reading socialism or the dogs did a better job looking after the herd. After that, E. A. hired a young man from Missouri to look after them. This young man, A. G. McKeen, had run a drug store until his health began to fail, and so he decided to hit for the country west of the Missouri where he could breathe that pure air and get well again. He herded for Morrison for years until E. A. decided to give up on sheep. McKeen always looked in good health when I saw him.

Morrison bought one of the first steam tractors in our country and broke quite a lot of prairie for himself and the other homesteaders. He had great hope for the disc-plow but in this tough sod it just wouldn't work. When Stanley County was divided, E. A. ran for commissioner along with twenty-three others. He was one of the three getting the highest number of votes cast, and so was elected to office. When Mrs. Morrison broke her hip in 1917, they moved to Philip, and he later served one term in the South Dakota Senate.

The Morrisons did a lot for the settlement of the country. They were always out in front trying new things, but didn't believe that the high range land was meant to be plowed up. That land should be used for cattle and sheep, E. A. used to say. He once told me about locating a bunch of homesteaders on the highest and driest land, hoping they couldn't find water and would have to go back where they came from. In his big pasture, he had some high and dry land, he thought, so he located Bill Runhol, a widower, and his seven children there, expecting them to pull up stakes when they couldn't find water. But he hadn't reckoned with old man Runhol being a water-witch and that he had the power of locating underground water with a forked stick. Well, Runhol walked around this high, dry land and where his forked stick turned down, he dug a well and got good water and plenty of it. He witched another well and found water again. The old man was a good farmer, not a stockman, he saved his money, and bought good machinery and even a silo. His daughter, Mary, did the housekeeping for the family. One of his boys still runs the place. E. A. says the laugh is on him. But Bill Runhol later shot a man, and then killed himself.

One time we had Runhol witch a well for us, and where his forked stick turned down, we started digging a well. Shy was running the windlass that pulled the half-barrel filled with dirt out of the hole and E. A. was down in the hole with the shovel. Shy's

50

hands got wet and the bucket slipped, hitting Ed on the head and knocking him out for awhile.

The Morrison children were as unusual as the parents. All four of them were graduated from South Dakota State College. Freda was about my age and when she was teaching school east of us she would stop on her way home and visit with me. After Stanley county was set up, she became Associate Club and 4-H leader and since our children were in 4-H club work, we worked a lot together. Joe Morrison was a club leader and worked with our boys a great deal. He had been at the Highmore Experimental Farm and helped develop a soft wheat. He raised some out here and gave each of the boys of the club a bushel to see what they could do with it. From that one bushel, we harvested twenty bushels. We raised that wheat here for quite awhile. It didn't bring the best price but it made up for it in yield. When Joe gave up club work, the boys bought him a gold watch. Years later, he pulled that watch out of his pocket and told me how much he valued it. Joe made two attempts to run his father's farm, but didn't do too well. He was too many years ahead of the country, believing in conservation, better livestock, bigger ranches, seed adapted to the dry country, and new methods for holding the moisture in the soil in the dry season.

"Doctor Morrison"

Sometime during the second winter we spent west of the Missouri, E. A. Morrison was on his way home from Ft. Pierre with a wagon load of freight. The road was heavy with snow and so he pulled into the Jud Robinson place to spend the night. The Robinson ranch was about twenty miles from the Morrison place. After putting up his team, E. A. went to the house and found the Robinsons very excited. Their first baby was about to be born. Jud had asked a woman to come over to help them but it looked as if she wouldn't get there in time.

Morrison knew that something had to be done and that pretty quick. Jud was all thumbs and couldn't possibly deliver a baby, his or anybody's. E. A. rolled up his sleeves, scrubbed up, and in short order helped the child into the world. He took care of the mother and baby as if he had done such things all his life. For a long time, people called him "doctor" and he got quite a kick out of it.

Not long after we had had a baby girl, after the run of boy babies, we were at a gathering at Wellsburg. Young Joe Morrison, who then lived on the Morrison ranch, was there showing off his baby girl. When he brought her over to me, instead of "oh-ing" and "ah-ing," I said, "She is sweet, Joe, but after you have had a half dozen the newness will wear off a bit." I was still feeling a little hurt at what Joe had said when someone asked him if he had heard the news, "The Fairchilds have a baby girl!" Joe's answer was, "That's not news. That's a yearly happening as regular as New Year's and the Fourth of July." After five boys in a row, I felt that a baby girl was news.

Fred Wells

I remember when Fred Wells came by our place looking for a claim. He had his son, Fred Jr., with him, but had left the rest of the family in Chicago where he had been running a milk route. That winter he and the boy dug a hole in the hillside, covered it with poles and hay, and lived there until they had a log cabin built. The family came out in the spring. None of them had ever lived in the country before, let alone out on the prairies in a dugout. He bought a team but didn't know how to hitch it up. One day I saw a team of bay horses coming down the trail, dragging a wagon tongue. They were running away. The tongue flew right and left, bumping their heels and scaring them to death. When they pulled into our hay corral, they got tangled up in the wire. They were covered with lather and trembling all over. I cut the wire away from their legs and got them loose. Fred had hitched them to a mower and they had got away from him.

When Wells went to Pierre in the spring to bring out his family, the wife and nine children, ranging in age from ten to twenty-three years made a full load for the wagon. But he put on a lot of supplies, too. This was too much for the team, so the family had to take turns walking along to lighten the load. When they got within a quarter mile of our place, two wheels dropped into a hole that was covered with snow. The horses were too exhausted to pull it out, so they had to unload everything. Wells sent ten-year old Nellie ahead to our house and asked me to get them a meal. They hadn't had much to eat since leaving Pierre. I can still see this little girl coming up to our house, carrying a doll twice as big as she was. She was shy, but when I opened the door she managed to say, "Daddy wants you to get us something to eat."

"Homesteaders in the Dakotas plant a beet seed in the spring close to the house, and in the fall they pull up the beet and brick up the hole for a cistern."

CHAPTER VI

Interesting People and Places

"When we burned cowchips for fuel, it took one person full-time just carrying them in and one person full-time just carrying out the ashes."

During the big rush for homesteads in 1906 and 1907, land agents with a bunch of what the cowmen called "the wool hat people" often stopped at our place to spend the night. I bedded them down for twenty-five cents a head on the floor and in our beds, and sent the family to the barn. I cooked them a good homesteaders' meal of meat and potatoes and spud varnish (as we called gravy) and charged them twenty-five cents, taking it as it came. We didn't exactly get rich at this, but it did give us some extra cash in the days when we didn't have very much. Some of these people took up claims around us and some moved on further west where the grass looked greener.

Preacher Tell

Preacher Tell came into our country in the early years and homesteaded west of Philip. He tried to do a little farming and preach in the little church at Philip on Sunday. He was a great lover of horses and often came out to our place. One time he spent the night with us, and for the first time Shy learned that he was a preacher and he was shocked. He always used a lot of cuss words, even when talking about good horses. To think that he treated this man as an ordinary person was pretty hard to take. But the preacher must not have minded since he came back later and got a team of Standard-bred geldings that Shy wanted him to break to harness. Mr. Tell must have had a way with horses, for in six months he was back with this high strung team and they were as gentle as lambs. He could drop the lines and leave them, and they would stand. He could pick up a foot and set it down and the horses would never move it an inch. They were so good and gentle that he bought them. Shy's Standard-bred stock was good and they always did well at the fair or when run at celebrations and picnics.

Barbed-wire Telephone Line

It was Preacher Davis that thought of linking the settlers together with a barbed-wire telephone line. He got this happy idea in 1908. His wife was alone on their claim quite a lot when he was gone and she needed some way of getting in touch with the neighbors. He installed a buzzer on the barbed wire fence and this made it possible for her to signal the nearest neighbor. Later, he put in a telephone at each place, connected by the barbed-wire line, and they could talk to each other. Why not link the whole country with a barbed-wire telephone line?

Mr. Davis came over to our house to see if we would go along with the idea. Shy didn't think much of it, but I did, and talked it up among the neighbors. Most of them weren't much interested, never having seen a telephone, but twelve of them agreed to go along with the plan. The cost was to be $13 and Preacher Davis would furnish the phones and put them in. After installing our phone, he went along the fence putting in high posts over section lines so the wire would not be grounded out, and tested every two miles. Some of the younger children went with me and helped with the equipment. Emma was left at home to answer the phone. She had been instructed how to answer when the bell sounded. This was a pretty exciting event for all of us. When she heard the bell, she ran to the phone and yelled "Hello," and then began to cry. The barbed-wire telephone was a miracle and it was too much for Emma. Needless to say, Shy never would have anything to do with it. Soon other neighbors wanted phones and this finally gave us a spider-web that stretched out close to 100 miles. The lines would carry about eight settlers and then there would be a switch put in. These eight might have twenty-five miles of wire to look

54

after. There weren't any hired telephone operators or trouble-shooters, but if the bells didn't ring, it was up to the people to get out and find the trouble. We later got a high-line switch and this connected us with Philip.

Elbon Store

Elbon was a little country store started by a homesteader named Noble, and when the post office was set up there, it was given his name spelled backwards. He sold out to Haakon Einan, another homesteader, who moved the place south a mile. This was the end of the line in our telephone system. If we called Philip, we had to go over the high line and had to pay toll. Later, we had a seven-way switch at Elbon.

Over the years, the store changed hands many times, so many that it wore itself out. When the Reeders owned it, the family of ten soon ate up the stock and so it was sold again. When Bill Runhol owned the place he got into trouble with his neighbors about some horses. He got so mad about it that he shot a man and then in remorse killed himself. By this time, the little store that had served the neighborhood for years, died a natural death.

Old Gebbes and the Party Line

Old Gebbes was the homesteader who had both a slew of kids and a telephone. Mrs. Gebbes worked outside in the fields a lot and left the young children alone in the shack. When they heard the telephone ring, they would grab the receiver and listen and make so much noise that no one else could hear. Once we spoke to Gebbes about it and I suppose he told the children to leave the phone alone, but the noise kept on. I decided to give them a taste of their own medicine the first chance I got. When we heard him call one of the neighbors, I told our family to keep as quiet as mice. I put the receiver to the mouthpiece which produced an ear-jarring whistling noise, then I rubbed wires together to make other weird sounds. In a few minutes he called up and said, "Mrs. Fairchild, I wish you would make your young ones stay away from the phone so I can talk." I said, "Mr. Gebbes, there isn't a bit of noise here in my house and my children aren't bothering the phone. If you are having trouble hearing, you now know how hard it is for others to hear when you are out of your house and your children are there alone." And that put a stop to the Gebbes racket.

Stephenson, the Hired Hand

Ed Stephenson came to our house when he was about seventeen and asked for work. Every now and then some man drifted by the place looking for a job until he could get a stake and file on a homestead. Ed was just getting over a big bender and was still pretty groggy. He sat around the house for a half day while Emma showed him pictures and talked to him. Shy asked if we should hire him and I said, "Well, you need help right now. Why not try him out tomorrow and see what he can do?" It turned out he was one of the best hands we ever had.

Ed was a hard worker but how he could cuss. Shy put him to work one day cleaning out the barn, and told him to use a team of a stallion and a thorough-bred mare. The stallion was slow and the mare was fast. When Ed told them to giddap, the mare would be off like a shot and the stallion would be riding on the scraper. He cussed them until the air was blue and I could hear him all over the place. I told Shy, "For Heaven's Sake, take that team away from that man. He's wearing himself out just cussing."

Another time he was chopping some firewood. Emma was teasing him by throwing some chips at him. He picked up a big chip and threw it at her. It hit her on the cheek and she went into the house bawling. Another time he ran over her with the wagon. He said he sure expected to get his walking papers every time something happened to Emma and it was a long way back to Minnesota where he came from.

After Ed had worked for us for two and a half years, he went to work for Pete Ulrey. When he was at our house he never did much drinking, but he got to hitting the bottle quite a lot over at Ulreys. One day he came over to our place and wanted to borrow a horse and wagon. We never asked any questions, just gave him what he wanted. He drove back to Ulreys at night, picked up their daughter, Jessie, and drove east of the river to Oneida where they were married. This caused quite a sensation. Ulrey came over to our place to see if we knew where Ed was, and that was the first we learned why he wanted to borrow the rig. In about ten days when the hue and cry died down, Ed brought his wife back to his homestead. Not long afterward, they were divorced. It is too bad that the marriage didn't last, especially since it had such a good start.

While Ed was building up his own place, he worked for us off and on, and later married Jessie Kouison. He went into the sheep business and in a few years built a fine modern home. They had three children who spent a lot of time over at our house playing with our young ones. Mrs. Stephenson said "I might as well pack their suitcases and let them live with you. They're there most of the time anyway." Later, the Stephensons sold their place and moved to Philip which in 1907 had been laid out as a railroad town.

Lena King, A Female Cowboy

The first year we were on the claim a rider dropped in one day and asked to feed his horse. He wore the usual Stetson hat, overalls, shirt, and boots, and was in need of a haircut. Before coming into the house, he spit out a cud of tobacco. We offered him a cup of coffee, and had quite a spirited conversation with him as he drank it. This visitor seemed to be well versed on about any topic I brought up, and I wondered how he ever learned all the things about keeping house. Even a bachelor cowboy wouldn't know very much about making bread and churning butter. When I asked him his name, he said, "I'm Lena King." You could have knocked me down with a feather. Lord knows, no one would have known that this cowboy was a woman. Her voice was heavy and she talked like a man. She was dressed like a man and looked like the cowboys that we often saw around our place.

As it was about supper time I invited her to stay and eat with us. She seemed glad to be invited. It had been a long day, she said, for she had been in the saddle since before daybreak and would welcome something to eat that didn't come out of a saddlebag. She had been looking for a lost horse and having found it, was now on the way home. She had picketed it out on the prairie before riding into our place. When I asked her to stay all night, she said she had to look after the horse. "That goddamned brute may tear his foot on the rope if I don't get him moving toward home," she added as she started west on her last lap of fourteen miles.

Over the years, I got to know Lena better. She could hardly read or write, yet she seemed to be well educated. Where she picked up all her information I could never find out. No matter what I asked her, she had an answer at her tongue's end. She had married a man much older than she was, a fellow who wasn't very practical and who spent a lot of his time dreaming. She had been forced to run the ranch about the way I had been. She herded cattle and horses, took care of the young stock, did the butchering and marketing, and even had to do the castration of the young bulls and stallions. Over the years, she built up a nice ranch and a good home. She didn't do any house work at all. It suited her husband to do the inside work while she ran the ranch. Lena felt more at home in a little camp shack off some place with the cattle.

One day I asked her, "Don't you like children?" "Oh, yes," she said, "when I get ready I'll give Bill a baby." About a year or so later when she had gone to Pierre with a bunch of cattle, word came to Bill at the home ranch that he was the father of a baby girl. He was so excited that he bought a new Dodge to bring the mother and baby home in style. Lena stayed at home for nearly a year nursing little Blanche. After they got to be yearlings, she said, children ought to be able to take care of themselves. Bill hired a housekeeper to look after the baby and Mama went back to her cows and horses.

Lena kept a good string of trading stock, and many a smart Alec got singed trading with her. When they tried to get even, they got singed even worse. One of our boys happened to be one of her victims. We had a good laugh about it, and didn't hold it against her. I'm sure that Lena was cleaner on the inside than on the outside even if she did do some sharp dealing.

Lena never seemed to be exactly a woman. When she stayed with us one night, I felt strange sleeping with her. When she pulled off her pants and shirt, and crawled into bed with me in her longjohn underwear, with the smell of chewing tobacco on her breath, I had a queer feeling that I was bedding down with a strange man. Stock buyers who came to her ranch had the same puzzled reaction. Some of them didn't know that she was a woman, and would relieve themselves while out looking at the livestock for sale. When they asked who to make the check to, she would say, "Lena King." "Who is Lena King?" She would say, "Me." Then it dawned on them that they had done some embarrassing things in the presence of a woman.

The years rolled by. The baby Blanche grew up and married. Lena and Bill decided they couldn't get along and so agreed to live apart. When she was telling me about it, she said, "I've given the son-of-a-bitch $1,000 to get off the place and never come back." The last time I visited with her, she was just coming from the hospital and I could see from her talk that she was not her usual self. I remember her saying that she wouldn't last long. She went home that night and threw herself on the bed without undressing — and died. When she was found a couple of days later, the rats had got to her. Somehow, it seemed to me that was not a fitting way for her to die. Her epitaph might have been: "She was as God made Her."

Hanging Wallpaper and Being Neighborly

One day Joe Morrison drove up to the house in his Model T Ford and said, "Could you come up and help Alice hang wallpaper? She has got to the corner and got stuck and is ready to bawl. I told Alice that if anyone could help her do the job, you could." Of course, with that kind of talk I would break my neck trying to be neighborly.

I gathered up the baby and went with Joe to the Morrison place. It didn't take long to size up the corner situation. The old burlap that had been nailed over the logs had to be stretched tight and tacked down. We loosened up the door casing and stuck in the blue building paper and tacked this down tight. I stayed all day and we got past the other two corners before it was time for me to get home to do the chores. Alice made me a pair of pillow cases as a remembrance of the day's wall papering, and I still have them after thirty years.

Joe's father was riding by our place in 1903 after Jasper was born, and came in to see the new six-day-old baby. When I opened the door, he said he was surprised to see me up and around and asked me why I was out of bed. "I am washing clothes and am in quite a mess," I said, "come on in." He asked where Shy was and I told him he was out riding some place. "Why isn't he here helping you?" he asked. That was an easy question, but I didn't give him the answer. Shy thought washing clothes was a woman's work and he would have nothing to do with it. I didn't expect him back until the washing was done and hung on the line.

E. A. was upset. He told me to sit down and to stay out of the draft — a pretty hard thing to do in that log house. He rolled up his sleeves, finished washing the clothes, hung them out, emptied the dirty water, all the time telling me how to take care of my health and why I shouldn't over-do so soon after having had the baby. "What might happen to all these little ones if you should die," he scolded. Shy rode in just as he was leaving, but E. A. didn't stop to give him advice on how to help his wife. It wouldn't have done any good anyway. But E. A. did his best deed when he got the Top Bar school started for the twenty youngsters that lived around there.

Calamity Jane in Ft. Pierre

It was ninety miles to Ft. Pierre, and freighters hauled goods from the end of the railroad there to the new settlements west of the Missouri. Fred Rowe's hardware store would send out things on time and we would pay for them when we sold some livestock, or when Shy went into Ft. Pierre to get a wagon load of lumber or a plow or other farm implements. Once when Shy was in Rowe's store, he saw Calamity Jane put on one of her exhibitions. When she came into the store, someone made a remark that she didn't like. Then she said something to the loafers there, pulled out her gun, and started shooting at their feet. She cleared the store in no time.

Olaf Aaen from Wisconsin

Among the people who moved out to South Dakota in these early years, there were a lot of young men trying to get a start in life by working for a homesteader until they could build up a spread themselves. Some of the early immigrants had lung trouble and hoped the dry air would bring them back to health. One of these young men was Olaf Aaen, who came from a Scandinavian family in Wisconsin. He had had pneumonia and one of his lungs had been removed. His other lung caused him some trouble and he also had to have a tube in his side. On his way west, he stopped at our place and asked if he could work for his board. We gave him a job, but didn't ask much of him, letting him do just what he felt like doing. He helped me with little jobs around the house and was a lot of company to me and the children. I never learned whether he got back his health in our dry climate or not.

Jim Louison brought his family out from Weyauwega, Wisconsin, hoping for better health. The children were pretty well grown up, and several of them also took up land. Louie's condition improved and his children got their start in life on free land in South Dakota. This was one case where the move west was a fortunate one.

Mr. Green and the Stage

Our place was a stop on the stage route from Ft. Pierre and the Black Hills. Orm Green carried the mail from Manila to Pedro for several years, and stopped with us for his dinner and to change horses six days a week. He used a democrat wagon and carried freight and passengers as well as mail. He paid me twenty-five cents a meal and also for feeding the six or eight horses he kept with us.

On one of these trips, a piece of harness broke just before he got to our place and the tongue fell down. The horses spooked and ran away. Just before this happened, he had taken a fresh chew of tobacco and was getting it softened up enough to enjoy the juice. When the six-horse team took off, leaving him and his wagon behind, he swallowed his cud. By the time he caught up with his horses, he was very sick, and spent the day just lying around our place. Maybe sleet and hail can't stop the mail, but a chew of tobacco can.

At another time, Mr. Green got sick before he started on the run, and he hired a young man to take it for him. It was early spring, the snow was melting, and the creeks were filled with water. When the young man drove his democrat wagon over our little creek, he missed the crossing, and the horses were carried down stream. The team was drowned but the young man got out alive. Some of the mail sacks were found six months later way down creek.

CHAPTER VII

Livestock and Rattlesnakes

"When the cattle and horses huddle at the end of the pasture and the bees stay in the hive, bad weather is on the way."

"You can expect a long, hard winter if the 'woolly bear' caterpillars have narrow instead of broad brown bands, if corn husks are hard to pull apart in the fall, and if skunks come early to make their lodging under the barn."

The bunch grass country west of the Missouri was a wonderful country for livestock. It was beautiful in the spring when the hills were green and the wild flowers were in bloom, and still beautiful in the fall when the grass was brown and the hills were golden. There were a few little streams and buffalo wallows where the cattle and horses could get water, stand in the mud, and stamp at the flies. But winters were hard and long, for both ranchers and livestock.

When the homesteaders moved in after 1902, they ruined the range for the cattlemen and sheepmen, for they located on water if they could and fenced their land to keep the range stock out of their fields. They plowed up the sod, planted enough crops to feed their animals, and if they stayed at it, became general farmers who

61

made their living with both livestock and crop land. Shy wanted to raise horses, and if he had had his way, the Fairchild brand "Flag S" would have been burnt only on horses, and such things as orchards and alfalfa would never have been a part of our ranch life. This was a hostile country to make a home in, even if the land was free. Hundreds of people who came out from the East soon gave up. We made it because we found a way to run a general farm in the dry prairies. But we had exciting times with the livestock — and rattlesnakes! They were even more interesting than some of the neighbors!

Tobe, the Horse that was a Nuisance

On a trip to Ft. Pierre, Shy picked up a two-year old gelding named Tobe. He had been a pet and a good kids' horse, but was a terrible nuisance around the place. He would chew tobacco, drink milk, and upset the slop pails. He had a habit of untying himself, always at the wrong time for us. On one trip, Shy was hauling a wagon load of grain. Tobe got himself untied during the night and scattered sack after sack of grain all over the ground.

One day after I had churned and set the buttermilk outside in a pail, Tobe came along and drank all of it. After dinner, I hitched him up and started to Marietta for groceries. I hadn't gone more than half a mile when Tobe lay down in the harness, with a stomach ache, I suppose, by the noises he made. I got him unhitched from the rig, got him up, and walked him around for awhile. It didn't take him long to get over his stomach ache and we got on our way. I don't remember if he ever stole the buttermilk again, but he continued to be a nuisance in many other ways.

Once when I was riding Tobe, he stepped in a badger hole and fell down. I kept in the saddle when he went down, but as he was getting up, he fell again, pinning my leg under him. No bones were broken but he rolled the flesh on my leg from hip to knee. The bruise was so bad that the blood vessels were blocked. Three abcesses formed and I was in great misery. At that time we were miles from a doctor and we had to do our own doctoring. Shy took his jack-knife and opened up one of the abscesses right above my knee. He probed the wound as far as the knife would reach but didn't seem to hit the right spot. I was suffering so much that we sent the hired man to the Indian reservation, forty-five miles away, where there was a woman doctor, but she would not leave the reservation, come hell or high water. She did send some medicine for me. But during the night when the hired man was gone, the abscess broke despite all that Shy had done with his jack-knife. What a relief! And Tobe was the cause of it all.

Red Durham Bulls

Most of the cattle west of the Missouri were a scrawny lot. They were a mix of everything from Texas Longhorns to scrub dairy cows and would not win many prizes in livestock shows. I knew that we had to get a good bull to breed up the stock if we were ever to have a decent herd.

We got a Red Durham bull and paid a high price for him. When we brought him home, he refused to eat grain. We had him less than a year and got one calf crop out of him, when something happened. He lost the use of his back legs almost completely. Since a bull that couldn't stand on his hind legs wasn't of much use, we decided to sell him. He weighed 2200 pounds and brought $102. Even if he did sire a few good calves before he was sold for baloney, he didn't exactly put the Fairchilds into the cattle business.

When a neighbor, Mr. Wilsey, came out from Missouri to homestead, he brought a good Red Durham bull with him. This animal was beautiful but he had a bad disposition. Wilsey used him for plowing, but decided to get rid of him after a few years and sold him to Mr. Radway. One day the bull got out and wandered over to the Maynard's place. Not knowing anything about his bad temper, Mrs. Maynard undertook to drive him off. He turned on her and nearly killed her before she could get up and run for the shed. She climbed up on the roof and the bull kept her there all day.

Shy decided that he would do some bull-swapping, trading our nice quiet bull to Radway for this mean one. He could handle this critter, he said. The new bull was brought home with a bunch of cattle and turned loose in the pasture. We had him a year and in that time no one was safe in the pasture whether he be afoot or on horseback. One day Shy got him in the barn and thought he could beat him until he got afraid of people. He knocked out one eye, but that didn't seem to make any difference. If anything, he was worse than he had been before. He could sense people a long way off and would start to beller and to paw before charging. I stood this as long as I could, worrying about the children getting over into the pasture, and told Shy either the bull had to go or I would. It was the bull that went to market. We were not breeding up our herd very fast.

Taming Wild Horses

When we took our homestead, the range had a lot of unclaimed horses on it, most of them being in the Badlands further west. Some of them were offspring of the Spanish strains that the

Texans had brought to the upper plains in the 1870's and 1880's and some were just ranchers' horses that had gone wild. A lot of little ranchers and homesteaders caught these animals, broke them, and made good saddle horses of them.

During a storm in the early spring, a range mare got separated from her colt not far from our place. Three or four days later, when we were riding after our stock, we found this little dogie wandering around all alone on the prairie. He wobbled up to the mare Shy was riding and followed him home. We put him on the bottle and named him Dickie. He never grew very big, weighing at most only 900 pounds. Having been raised by hand, he was as tame as a dog, and the youngest children rode him everywhere.

After we got a Sunday School started, we tried to get the children there whenever it was held. One Sunday there were no horses up for them to ride to Sunday School, so Shy hitched up Dickie to the buggy. He had never been hitched up before but seemed not to be excited about having a rig behind him. There were five children scrubbed and dressed up, ready to go. Emma, the oldest, got in and took the lines. Two others sat with her and two stood behind. They were barely out of the yard when one of them stood up in the seat — to show off a little, no doubt — and this scared Dickie. Emma held on to the lines and pulled him around in a circle a time or two. Shy went out to help and got between the wheels, thinking he could brace himself and stop the horse. But Dickie had heard the call of the wild, and off he went. Emma jumped out the back. Only Clint stayed in the buggy until Dickie ran into the gate and stopped. When we asked Clint why he hadn't jumped out, he showed his trust in his old pet: "Why, Dickie wouldn't hurt me."

Prairie Girl was another colt we picked up on the range and raised by hand. She was full of mischief and gave me all sorts of trouble. She followed the children around for her bottle and if they didn't watch out, she would slip into the house when they left the screen door open, and nose everything off the table looking for milk. We just had to build a fence around the yard to keep her away from the house. The children rode and drove her and she was their old standby saddle horse for years.

Another wild one we found was Chet. He was so unpredictable that it wasn't safe for a bronc-buster to mount him. One day we got him in the corral, made a dummy and tied it on him, and turned him loose to buck to his heart's content. Then Ed Stephenson, the hired man, got on and rode him.

One evening Ed was a little under the weather with some Dakota Tanglefoot. It was nearly night when he came into the barn and saw the dummy. He was too far gone to realize that the dummy was not a person. I heard him cussing and taunting "him" to come out with his fists up. This went on until I yelled at him, asking him what was the matter. When he learned about his mistake, he looked pretty sheepish.

We had a lot of fun with the dummy. When Jasper agreed to break a horse for Mr. Teeters, the dummy was used again. Jasper first tried to ride this bronco, but he got bucked off or nearly so every time. He decided to put the dummy on the horse and let it break him. Somehow the horse managed to get the corral gate open and galloped out to join a bunch of broke saddle horses in the pasture. Seeing a horse and dummy-rider coming after them, they took off for the corral. The wild one drove them out again, around and around the pasture, until they were pretty well tuckered out. Jasper got on another horse, cut the bronc and dummy out of the bunch, and ran him into Pfeiffer's corral. He had been tipped off that this critter was a bad rodeo horse that had been trained to buck. He managed to ride him over to Teeters and delivered him there, broke. "I can ride him now, so I suppose you can, too," he told Teeters as he collected his $5 right then and there. Stanley Teeters decided to mount, but he didn't stay long. The horse threw him over the fence and into some thistles. Mr. Teeters just chuckled. He knew all the time that the horse was a sour apple.

When Shy went out to our claim early in 1902, he took along a beautiful Percheron stallion, ten other horses, and four Poland China brood sows in the emigrant car. He never got the stallion out to the ranch after unloading in Pierre. A horse rancher named Walden offered to trade two geldings and eight mares for the stallion, and Shy swapped right there. He used the mares as trading stock to build up our herd of cattle, but kept the geldings, Dan and Dave. All in all, I think he got around thirty-five head of cattle for these mares, counting the calves, cows, and yearlings. Walden turned the stallion out with a bunch of mares. Having always been stabled, he was no match for a range stallion that wanted the harem, and in the awful fight he was just torn to pieces and killed. It was such a shame, for he was a real beauty.

Pigs and Me

The first little pig we ever had on the place came from the Kurtzmans. Mrs. Kurtzman had been with me when one of the babies had come and I had made her take $10 for her help. She wasn't very happy about taking anything since she knew that homesteaders had to help each other. One time when we were over there visiting, she took us out to see their sow and her litter of pigs. When I was looking at the pigs, I said that I wished to goodness that we could get hold of a pig to drink up some of the milk we were throwing away. She said to her husband, "Pete, jump over the fence and get one of the little pigs for Mrs. Fairchild to take home." He picked up one by the tail, so it wouldn't squeal, and handed it to me. I was in the pig business!

What a pest that pig was! She would sneak in the open screen door quicker than the kids, and just as fast, and turn over the slop pail. I cleaned up many a mess after her. She was raised on milk, and never had any grain, but that fall we enjoyed eating pork instead of beef.

When I was growing up in southern Wisconsin, little did I know that I was learning a lot of things about nature that would help me when I settled on a Dakota homestead. When the brood sows that Shy took out had their first pigs, they were so fat that they couldn't deliver them. Two had died before I decided to play midwife myself. My hands were small enough to reach in and get hold of the pigs without hurting them. On the first try I took a little rope in my hand and put it on the lower jaw of a little pig and pulled it out. This worked and so I kept on until I had delivered all the pigs. The two sows lived, too.

Calves and Me

Over the years, I served as a midwife for pigs, calves, and babies. I didn't cringe from things like that, for it seemed to me that saving life was more important than being squeamish about it. Many a time I helped neighbors when they had trouble with their stock as well as when I helped bring their children into the world.

I remember one time when I wondered about taking on the job. We had a two-year old heifer that seemed awful weak and we had kept her in the corral to watch her. One day Shy left the gate open when he rode off on to see one of the neighbors, and the heifer got out. I saw her going toward the creek but being afoot, I couldn't stop her. There by the creek she lay down and started having her calf. I gave her plenty of time but the calf did not come. Finally, I twisted her tail, got her up, and tried to drive her up to the house, but she was in such pain that she ran for the waterhole, and fell down. I waded in, pulled her around and got her head above water. After resting awhile, she got up and let me lead her to a tree where I tied her. The calf's head was showing, but this is not the natural way for a calf to be born. It looked bad for the heifer.

I sent one of the boys over to Charlie Sears for some help. Charlie was a bachelor, but he was a stockman and surely knew something about calving. I knew he was shy, so I kept out of sight while he tried to see what he could do for her. After awhile he came to the house, said that he couldn't do anything. I said, "Charlie, if it doesn't bother you too much I'll go with you and we will see what can be done about it." I took some small ropes and some wire with me. I pushed the head back and tried to get hold of the calf's feet, but the feet were both backwards. There was nothing left to do but cut off the calf's head. I took a knife and cut off the head, reached in and got a rope tied on to the feet, and we pulled the calf out and we saved the heifer. It was not unusual for two-year olds to have trouble with their first calves.

The word got around that Grace Fairchild was a pretty good veterinarian. Often I was called on to help deliver calves and colts and pigs, as well as babies, and I never refused. Teaching sex to the children wasn't much of a problem in our circumstances.

After we had been on our place twenty-five years or so, and had as many hogs as we could take care of, Shy went to a sale one day, and came home with four more sows, soon to have pigs. "Got 'em dam cheap," he said. Right off the bat we learned they were chicken eaters, so we penned them. The first sow to have her pigs ate all of them before we knew anything about it. We took two pigs away from the second one before she could eat all of them. We turned the other two sows in the pasture, watched them carefully, and managed to save their pigs. A few days later, I heard a pig squeal and ran to see what was the matter. I found that the two sows we had penned up had got out and found the other sows down in the grove and had eaten six of the eight pigs in one litter. I called for help and the boys got them back in the pen. I wondered how they got out. Both doors were open. A sow couldn't push the latch and open the door. Shy finally admitted that he had let the sows out to get some green grass and exercise. I think we may have got our money back for the four sows when we fattened them up and sold them, but a lot of work and grief and plain disgust went into that "dam good buy."

Rattlesnakes

It is a good thing that I have never been afraid of snakes, for if I had been, I don't believe that I could have stayed on our homestead. On our way out from Ft. Pierre in 1902, we killed several and over the years I collected half a cigar box full of rattles. Then we quit saving them. Killing a rattler wasn't even news, but we never let it escape if we could possibly prevent it.

The first summer on the ranch was hot as blazes most of the time. On a real scorching day — a hot sun and not a breath of air moving — I set the baby out in the shade, propped her up with pillows, and went back into our little log house to do my work. I

67

could hear her cooing and now and then would look out at her. Suddenly, it dawned on me that Leah wasn't cooing any more and must have fallen asleep. I went out to see if she was, and what I saw petrified me. About three feet from her was a big rattler, all coiled and ready to strike. Quickly, I reached down and pulled her out of danger, and killed the snake. I looked the baby over but couldn't find any signs of a bite. Then, a chill came over me and I shook with fright. What would have happened to Leah if she hadn't stopped cooing?

A few days later, we saw another big rattler trying to get under the house. I killed it, and thought it looked like a mate to the other one I had killed. In the fall, we killed a lot of rattlers around the buildings. We thought they were migrating for the winter to a prairie dog town a quarter of a mile east of the house. On nice fall days we saw a lot of snakes sunning themselves around the prairie dog village and managed to kill many of them before they could crawl into a hole.

One evening when I was after the cows, I saw a rattler crawling along the path leading to the corral. It didn't coil up when it saw me, but seemed to be on its way somewhere. I didn't have a club with me but didn't want it to get away. Even if the path led through a cactus bed, I decided to take off my shoes and try to stun it with a shoe. I threw my shoes at it until I got him hurt, then I thought of my long hat pin. I stuck the pin through his head, pinned him down to the ground, and finished him off with the heel of a shoe.

Once when my sister Leona was visiting us, she and I decided to look for some wild grapes. We went horseback and on the way saw a rattler. I didn't have anything to kill it with, so I took the heavy sack we had for grapes, threw it over the snake and tramped on it until it stopped moving. Than I took off the sack and finished the job with the heel of my shoe. After living for awhile in this rattlesnake country, I learned never to leave the house without carrying a stick when on foot or a rope when on horseback.

Just before Thanksgiving one year, we almost had a runaway because of some rattlesnakes. Most homesteaders liked to go to church so when a missionary preacher, Mr. Davis, came to preach at Wellsburg, a little settlement four miles from us, we went to hear him. We were driving along in the buggy on the way home when all at once the team stopped and tried to turn around, almost upsetting the buggy. It took me awhile to get them settled down, and then I looked to see what had scared them. There on a prairie dog hole was a batch of snakes so entwined in each other that they looked like a braided rug. I unhitched the team, and took out the buggy whip and started in on the snakes. I whipped at them until I had all of them stunned and then I finished them off with the neck yoke. When I counted them, I had sixteen, ranging from one foot in length to three feet. We went on home and had dinner, and then we went back to the prairie dog village. Jasper was swinging his spade along and cut one in two without knowing it. I had heard it rattle but he hadn't. He cut it in two just as I called out to him that I heard one rattling. We killed twenty-eight all together, not a bad day's work. If we had sold the rattlesnake fat, we might have paid off our debt.

One day Shy brought in a little live rattler between the jaws of his pliers. It was about seven inches long but could rattle like the big ones. There was a big bump along in the middle of it which made it so big it couldn't crawl. We opened it up to see what was in it and found a mother mouse full of little mice. How that little snake managed to swallow such a mouthful was a mystery to me. The children learned about the "birds and bees," even from rattlesnakes.

One of our saddle horses, May, a standard-bred that had come out in the emigrant car, was a great one to spook every chance she had. She dumped most of us at one time or other, or made us pull leather in order to stay on. Usually we couldn't see anything that might have caused her to jump aside so fast. Once when Shy was riding her, she almost threw him. He thought old May had shied at a tumbleweed and decided to give her a lesson or two. He whipped her and tried to get her to go near the tumbleweed, but she refused to go. Then he got off and tried to lead her. She pulled back and danced around. He kicked her in the ribs and filled the air with cuss words, but still she refused to budge. After he had played himself out, and the horse, too, and they were farther from the tumbleweed than when he started, he stopped for breath. Then he heard a rattle and the noise came from the tumbleweed. He looked and saw a big rattlesnake and killed it with a rock. It was an old one with ten rattles and a button. This taught Shy a lesson. After that when May shied, he never argued with her, and let it go at that. If she could have separated the tumbleweeds with rattlers under them from tumbleweeds with nothing under them, she would have been a wonderful horse. But we kept her anyway until she was so old we put her out to pasture. All of us covered a lot of ground on her as long as we stayed in the saddle.

Frontier Woman

We camped in the middle of a rattlesnake settlement once when we were taking a bunch of cattle in to Ft. Pierre. Clyde Daley was to join us on the road with his bunch, and we were to put them in a deserted homesteader's corral along the way when we stopped at night. It was around November 1 and beginning to get cool on the prairies. We built our fire and cooked our supper, and had gone to bed on the ground in the homesteader's shack when Clyde got in with his cattle. We got his herd in the corral and he ate some of the food we had left over, and then he crawled under the covers on Shy's side.

The next morning we went on into town, and after selling the cattle, loaded our wagon with groceries and things we needed, and headed for home. About five miles out of town, the wagon lost a tire — the steel band that encased the wheel. Another wagon came by so Shy threw the wheel in and went back to town, and I stayed with the teams. He managed to get another wheel and to get back out to our wagon, but it was too late to go on that night. So we made camp near Welche's place, spread our bedding on the ground, and went to bed. The next day some people came out from town to check on the rattlers around there. A couple of boys had told around that they had killed two rattlers by the old dugout. Before they left, they had killed sixty snakes around our camp. It makes me shudder even now when I think of it.

Plain, Ordinary Snakes

We had more than rattlesnakes in South Dakota. Hardly a day went by in the summertime but that we didn't see a plain, ordinary garter snake, a bull snake, or around the waterholes, water snakes. When my mother lived on her homestead across the creek from us, she said one day that she wanted to pick some choke cherries. All of us got hungry for fruit and choke cherries helped meet the hunger. As we picked the cherries along the creek, we thought we heard a child crying. That didn't seem possible since we had my babies with us. We followed the sound down to the waterhole and could hear a weird cry coming from there. We looked awhile, then saw a water snake swallowing a garter snake. The water snake would gulp and squeeze, and from the look in its beady eyes, it seemed to be choking to death. It might have got the garter snake down but I doubt it. I took hold of their tails and pulled them apart. The garter snake was still alive and it swam away from us as if nothing had ever happened. The water snake took off downstream. I have heard about two snakes swallowing each other until nothing was left, but I never heard anybody explain how a snake could cry like a baby.

70

We always looked upon a bull snake as a friend. They weren't poisonous and they did do away with a lot of mice around the buildings. They were hard on birds and sometimes sucked hen's eggs. Sometimes it got exciting when I reached in a hen's nest and found a bull snake there instead. We had a hen that laid its eggs in a clump of tall grass not far from the house, but the nest was usually empty. After several trips there without finding an egg, I finally caught the culprit, a five foot bull snake, in the act of swallowing an egg. His jaws were so far apart that they looked to be unhinged. I picked him up and squeezed the egg out of him without breaking it. He was making a crying noise the way the water snake did. I carried him down to the creek and tossed him in, but he was back right away stealing eggs out of the nests. When I had to choose between one bull snake and eggs, I stood up on the side of the eggs. It is too bad I killed him for he probably got more mice, rats, and gophers than the eggs were worth.

One morning we heard the blackbirds making a commotion in the trees and saw them diving down on a nest in the limbs of the big cottonwood. They were kicking up quite a storm and I knew something was wrong. I sent Byron up the tree. As he started out on the big limb, he stopped short. Ahead of him was a big bull snake lying there stretched out, not much worried about the blackbirds flying around. Byron nearly fell out of the tree, he was so surprised. He picked up the snake and dropped him to the ground. Then we saw what he had been up to, for he had several bulges and bulges meant birds, we thought. We killed him and opened him up and found five baby blackbirds. Two of them were still alive but soon died.

Our children looked upon all snakes, except rattlers, as friends. They carried them around and for all I know, may have named them. Russell, especially, thought it foolish for anyone to be afraid of snakes. He would take a snake to school, let it crawl out of his pocket or pant's leg, and let it wiggle along on the floor. The children would scatter but Russell would stay at his desk studying as if nothing had happened. It's a wonder the teacher didn't send him home for good.

One night when he was a little older, Russell took his girlfriend to a dance. Out on the floor, a snake stuck its head out of his shirt. His girl screamed, and dragged him across the floor. He put the snake in the back of the car and came back to the dance. When they went to get in the car later, his girl saw the snake on the cushion and screamed again. This might be a good way to care for bull snakes, but it was a poor way to get along with a girl.

71

Russell never lost an interest in snakes. Whenever we saw a few rats around, Russell got his bull snakes on the job, headed them down the rat holes, and in no time, the place was cleaned up. A bull snake under the house was a good way to keep the rats and mice away, but we never liked to have them in the house itself.

One time, Mrs. Stephenson was at our place and saw a snake coming out of the bedroom. She gave a scream and ran home. But that was an accident. We didn't mind having bull snakes outdoors but there was a limit to where they were free to roam. It was the rattler that we feared, and we killed them by the hundreds. On the prairie, a settler learns his friends and his enemies and the sounds and habits of each one.

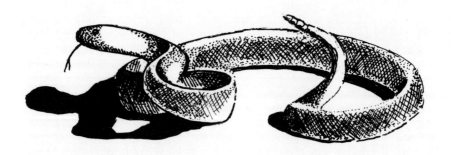

CHAPTER VIII

Never a Dull Moment

"The land was so rich that one rancher got twenty-six bushels per acre, all volunteer — he never planted a single grain."

"Pumpkins could be raised in South Dakota but the vines grow so fast that they wear the pumpkins out dragging them around on the prairie."

Some of the homesteaders who came out to Dakota to get rich found life hard and monotonous with one day's work followed by a similar one. There was a lot to do on our place, building our house bit by bit, having a baby every year or two, cooking, sewing, and looking after the livestock. It was a big enough job when a husband and wife work at it, but on our place, I had to do more and more of the work around the ranch. Shy always said he was sick and he never had much interest in anything but horses. Now I realize that he was too old to be a pioneer when he went out in 1902, and too much of a dreamer ever to stay at the job of proving up on a claim. Life was hard, but there was always something happening. I loved living on a homestead after I got settled down; he let it lick him. I only wish that we might have had a bigger dream than we did.

Coyotes were Pests

In the first year or two on the claim, I got some chickens and a few turkeys and looked forward to eggs and fried chicken and even Thanksgiving turkey. But it was hard to keep the pests away from them when we didn't have chicken-wire fences and coops to keep them in. We picked up a couple of dogs the second year and they helped keep the varmints away.

One morning I saw a coyote south of the house. This was not unusual since about every day we could see them loping on the ridge across the river. The little dog went out to tackle the coyote and the coyote took him on. I heard the fight and let the big dog out and he took off after the coyote. About that time, two more coyotes came on the scene and jumped on the big dog. Hair flew in all directions and the growls and yelps sounded terrible. I ran out and started yelling at the coyotes but the fight kept on. Lo and behold, I looked up and there were two more coming to join up with the three already mauling our dogs. About then, they got the signal and took off for the creek. Our dogs were surely anti-coyote after that, but our chickens had to stay in close or they'd be picked off.

Shy and his son Fred saw eight coyotes in a bunch one day, and took after them on horseback. They shot five of the eight, but that still left three to grab off chickens, baby lambs, calves, and even colts. Over the years we shot them, trapped them, and poisoned them, but there always seemed to be a fresh supply. As late as the 1930's, we still had too many coyotes. That fall I had fifty-odd turkeys weighing about six to eight pounds. They ran north of the house just out of sight. One day I heard a commotion and ran out to see what was happening. There was a coyote jumping and killing right and left. I called to the boys in the barn for help. While they got their horses saddled, I watched the coyote eat a turkey, and it made me sick. By the time the boys got organized, twenty-three turkeys lay dead, and the coyote had made his way back to his den somewhere out on the prairie.

One night in the 1930's I was awakened by a racket again among the turkeys. They were flying and gobbling and trying to get away from something. I jumped out of bed half asleep and could see a coyote after them. I called Wayne and we jumped into the old car without many clothes on and started out to run it down. But it had disappeared when we got out there. We drove up and down draws but couldn't find hide nor hair of the varmint. Maybe it had gone south toward the school, we thought, so we drove down there and sure enough we saw not one, but four. We took after the first one and ran it in a circle. While I drove, Wayne got the gun ready, and shot at it a couple of times, hitting it each time. Still it ran on. The box of shells was in the bottom of the car where Wayne couldn't reach them. With the gas pedal touching the floor and me driving in circles over rough ground, it was not easy for me to reach down underneath the seat to get the shells. But I did get hold of one, and Wayne loaded his rifle and killed the coyote. The others made a run for the creek. I was a wreck and darn near frozen, but pretty well satisfied that one coyote wouldn't be bothering the turkeys again.

Along about this time, Wayne was looking after the sheep afoot not far from the house. I heard him yell, wanting me to bring him the car and a gun. He had seen a coyote fooling around the sheep. I hollered at the hired man and we got the car out and off we went to take it to Wayne. He drove it seventy miles an hour over bumps and snow drifts, all the time keeping the coyote in sight. The hired man got in a shot but missed. We were headed for the creek so I yelled to Wayne to stop. He said he couldn't. We went into the swale, rolled over and over and landed on our wheels again. The gun, still cocked flew through the window. The hired man got a cut on his head. Wayne hung on to the wheel and was unhurt while I must have rolled around the back seat like a pumpkin and finished up jammed between body and door. I had three broken ribs and was bruised from top to bottom, and the car was a wreck. Wayne got the car pulled out of the hole and towed in to town. He paid the repair bill of $100. After that, I lost my yen to chase coyotes in a car, but I never could get friendly with them. They took our profits for too many years.

My Friend, the Skunk

In our early years, the boys trapped skunks and rabbits and sold the skins for spending money, and after the country was organized, trapped both magpies and coyotes for the bounty. But it was skunks that caused me a lot of trouble, but in a different way than coyotes, though skunks did kill some chickens for me.

Passing an old shack one day, Jasper looked down and saw some skunk signs and a hole under the building. He rushed home for a spade, the rifle, and some help. Back at the shack, he turned the corner and there was a skunk on its way out to look around the world. Doing what comes naturally, the little striped animal heisted his tail and squirted Jasper full in the face. Jap fell back, and yelled for help. The spray had blinded him and he had to be led home. His face turned red, and he stank to high heaven. It was a long time before we smelled the last of that skunk around the place.

75

Frontier Woman

Skunks still get under my house, but I let them alone. Not long ago something disturbed them and my house smelled of what we used to call polecat for a long time. I tried to kill them with monoxide gas from the car exhaust. I backed the little Crossley up to the house, hooked on the vacuum cleaner hose to the exhaust pipe, and pushed the nozzle under the house. In a few days there was a terrible stink in the house, but I couldn't tell whether it was dead skunk, rat, or weasel since all have been under the house at one time or another.

The boys discovered a nest of baby skunks beside the hay wagon and Joe thought it would be fun to raise them for pets. He sneaked up on them and grabbed two by the tail, lifted them up as fast as he could, and held them at arms length while the boys admired the pretty kittens. But Joe forgot that a skunk can spray whenever he has a foothold. One of the little kittens got his front feet on the wagon wheel and that was all he needed. He let loose with all that he had and that was enough to scatter the boys. Joe yelled "Cripes" and ran. They all decided that skunks might not make very good pets around the house after all. For a long time after this, we didn't think even boys were good to have around.

Shooting Coyotes and the Death of Little Leah

Life on a homestead was more than chasing coyotes and getting rid of skunk smells. We were a long way from a doctor and this meant that I had to do about all the doctoring that we had done. I had learned some remedies in my Wisconsin home, but in the years we raised a family in South Dakota I learned a lot more. We were always having accidents and most of them seemed to come when somebody was visiting us. The worst one we ever had was the shooting of little Leah in 1908. I always felt that Shy was to blame for this.

It was Shy's belief that he did not need to do anything until he was good and ready. He didn't want to be crowded by anyone. It was harvest time in 1908 when our hired man, Leo Hagler, had told us that he was quitting at a certain time and was going down to the Sand Hills of Nebraska to file on some land. Leo told Shy that since it took two men to stack wheat, he would help get that done before he left. But Shy kept putting it off and there was still one stack to do on the day that Leo had to leave. It looked stormy, so Shy said he would pitch the load on if I would pitch it off at the stack. I was not very happy about this because I thought he had had time to get it done when Leo was here, and that I had enough to do cooking and sewing and milking and working with the chickens and turkeys. Why should he have to use me as a hired hand in the field? We had six children, the oldest was eight, and I never left them alone unless some grown-up was there.

A few days before Leo left, my cousin, Augusta Nye Adams, and her thirteen year old son came to visit us a few days. It seemed safe to leave the children with them. Besides I would be working within sight of the house. Before I went to the field, Augusta and I went to the garden to get some vegetables. The boy had asked me the day before if we had a gun and if he could use it, and I had told him it was too big and dangerous for him. While we were in the garden he got the gun down and showed the children how to load it. When we got back from the garden the children were all sitting around so quietly I wondered what they had been up to. He had told them not to say anything about the gun. I went on to the field and that was a mistake.

While I was stacking, I looked toward the house and saw Emma running toward us, crying and yelling. When she got close enough, we heard her say that she had shot Leah. We stopped work and went to meet her, and ran on to the house. There we found little Leah dead, shot through the stomach. The children had been playing coyote and had done the way they had seen the grown-ups do when they got the gun and shot at them. They took turns being coyotes and being the person with the gun. In their befuddled little minds, they had finally loaded the gun, and when it was Emma's turn, she had shot her little sister.

Shy went off with horses on the run to get Mrs. Hampton to come down, yelling at the top of his voice, calling on God to forgive him. The Hamptons spread the word among the other settlers and they came in to help us, bringing food and the comfort of their friendship. Preacher Davis was in the neighborhood and he came over right away. He offered to go to Philip to get the wooden casket and to report to the county officials that the death was an accident. It was August and very hot so we packed the little body with ice from our own ice-house until we could make arrangements for the funeral. We buried her on a hill in sight of the house where she might look down on us with her merry smile.

I could forgive Shy for not being very practical and not having what it took to homestead a country where drought and grasshoppers and hard work were a part of life and only the strongest could survive. After all, at 48 maybe he was too old to be a homesteader when he went out in 1902. But I could never forgive him for putting off the wheat stacking so long that I had to be a hired hand and leave the young ones.

77

Accidents

With all the horses and cattle around the place, it is a wonder that we didn't have a lot more bones broken from kicks and falls than we had. All of us fell off horses, were kicked by cows, and pushed against the corral at catching-up time, but Byron seemed to be the child who was accident-prone. He broke his arm when he was four, and this caused a real crisis since bone-setting was a little beyond me.

The accident happened when our six-year old Clint was riding a gentle pony around the yard. Byron opened the gate and Clint's pony went out of the yard into a bunch of horses standing there under the trees. Byron tagged along. Shy had gone into town that morning and the horses he had brought up to the corral hadn't yet scattered out over the pasture. Before I knew what was going on, I heard Byron screaming bloody murder and I knew that something bad had happened to him. I ran to get him and saw the bone sticking through the flesh of his little arm. One of the horses had kicked him. I carried him to the house and bound his arm in a towel soaked with cold water, then hurried to the barn, caught up a team and hitched them to the buggy. We loaded up and off we went to Louie Johnsons to get some help. He got in and took the reins while I held Byron. He whipped the team most of the way to Philip and we made the twenty-five mile trip in two and a half hours. While Louie took care of the team, I carried Byron to Dr. Wycliff's office.

Shy had just got into town and was unhitching when Louie pulled into the livery barn. "I-I-I b-brought your w-w-wife d-d-down. One of the c-c-children g-g-got h-h-hurt." Shy ran for the doctor's office. By that time, the doctor was setting the bone and Byron was screaming for all he was worth. Shy was so scared that he swallowed his cud of tobacco, got pale, and ran out of the office.

After the doctor had the bone set, the arm started swelling and the muscles began to tighten up. I was still holding the boy's arm and noticed something wrong. I thought the bone had slipped a little and told the doctor that he had better try setting it again. Sure enough, one arm was an inch shorter than the other, so we had to do the whole thing over again. Poor Byron, he yelled and thrashed around, and I had to hold him by force while the doctor worked on the arm. His father just sat there retching.

The next day we put Byron on the buggy seat and headed for home. By the time we got near our place Byron was tired and restless. Shy would say to him, "You'll soon be home now," and

Byron would say, "Oh, shut up." This was not the last time that the boy got kicked by a horse or the last time that I took him to a doctor.

A few years later, we had more horse trouble. My sister Leah was visiting me so we might have known we would have some accident. We had brought a bunch of horses home from pasturing over on Spotted Bear Creek. Among them was a three-year old mare that had never been handled. I'll never know why that imp of misery, Byron, decided he had to rope this horse and put a surcingle on her. He put on an old pair of spurs which someone had left there, and climbed on. He had no more than touched her back than I saw his heels in the air, but he hung on to the surcingle for dear life. When he came down, the mare wasn't there. She whirled around and kicked him just as he lifted his head to get off of the ground. Her long sharp hoof hit him just below the lip, cutting through and taking out the four lower teeth as slick as a whistle. We didn't know how bad it was. All we could see was blood all over everything, and that the poor boy couldn't close his mouth. This kind of doctoring was beyond me.

We had the old Dodge car then so we headed for Pierre and the hospital there, ninety miles away. We didn't think that the dentist in Philip could put teeth back in or fix up a jawbone. We had quite a time getting to Pierre. The radiator leaked and we had to stop at every puddle for water. We got to the hospital in the middle of the night, but Dr. Riggs wasn't due until morning. The nurses kept Byron's jaw in a cold pack so it wouldn't swell so much by morning. When Dr. Riggs came he sat on the bed and gave him enough ether to put two boys under, and got him to sleep. Then he cut away the teeth from the flesh, bound up the jaw, and said he wanted him there for a few days just to see how he got along. Byron got along all right, never had any scar, but he had to wear a four-tooth bridge the rest of his life. It's a wonder we ever raised that child.

When Emma was about three years old, a neighbor's horse kicked her and opened up the upper lip. While the family held her, I took one stitch in the lip and closed it up. There is a little scar left. Chances are I should have taken two stitches.

Emma had another scar on her cheek. She and Leah usually played together without much trouble. One time when they were cutting out pictures they got into a scuffle over the scissors, and Emma ended up with two holes in her cheek. I didn't sew them up and so she will carry the scar to her dying day.

One winter when I was living alone, around 1940, I had to doctor myself. It had been a hard winter with a lot of snow, and the pheasants were starving to death because they couldn't get through the snow to the ground. Wayne was feeding sheep at our place and was hauling hay out to them. When the pheasants saw him coming, they would leave the trees and go over to the feeding place and pick up hay seed. Seeing all these pheasants, I decided to shoot a few of them for a good meal.

I got into the barn with the shotgun before the pheasants got up to the feeding place. When they came up, I got a bead on one but when I went to take off the safety catch it wouldn't move. I finally got it off, but forgot to hold the stock tightly between the thumb and index finger of my right hand. But I did have it tight against my shoulder. When I fired, the gun kicked upward, and my thumb was caught by the safety device and laid my thumb right back over my hand, ripping the flesh about three inches. I was so disgusted at not getting a pheasant that I didn't notice that I was bleeding like a stuck hog. When I saw the blood I set the gun down and went to the house, forgetting all about the pheasants. Besides, they had taken off when I shot. I pulled my thumb back in place and tried to make the tape hold the wound together, but it wouldn't work. So I got myself a needle and thread and sewed up the opening. I was ashamed of my work. I never told Wayne and since he was living at the other place, it was several days before I talked to him. When he came to the house a few days later and I asked him to take off the bandage, he yelled, "Jesus Christ, how did you do that?" I had him take out the stitches and wrap it up again. He said he would milk for me but I told him "I have been doing it all right along. I guess I can do it the rest of the time."

To cure the ordinary aches and pains, we used the old tried-and-true remedies: onion poultices for chest colds, boiled onion for ear ache, gargled kerosene for sore throat, Epsom salts for stomach ache and punctured feet, turpentine and kerosene for lice in hair, snow for frost bite, grease for burns. But it was good food, fresh air, and hard work that kept us healthy. The kids did not pretend they were sick even to get out of work when they knew that they would get a dose of Epsom salts.

Stagecoach Runaway

In the summer of 1906, my sister Leona Wayne Huxtable, and her two children visited us for a month. She had been sick for a long time and weighed only eighty-five pounds. She thought the dry air might cure her.

Leona came out from Ft. Pierre on the stagecoach pulled by three teams strung out ahead. Two of the horses were broncs and hardly broken, and they were put in the middle. The middle team was green. The driver was drunk! What a way to travel! The driver decided to quiet the horses down by letting them run. This was something new to Leona and she was scared to death as they rolled and rocked along. They made the forty-five miles to Hayes in no time. There they spent the night. The next morning the driver was still too drunk to hitch up the teams, so the livery stable boy did it. He took off the green teams used the day before but put the new lead horses on the tongue. They didn't know how to work on the tongue and nearly upset the rig, so the passengers had to get out and help change the horses around where they belonged. When Leona got to our place that night, she was worn out. Her first trip west of the Missouri in a stagecoach was harder on her than the one was on me when I made it with a wagon load of lumber in 1902.

During her visit with me, Leona's little nine-month old girl, Eva, had a fit. Leona pretty nearly had a fit, too. Neither one of us knew what to do for a baby having a convulsion. We called the hired man from the barn. He took one look, and got on a horse and rode after Shy who was fixing fence. I knew that Shy wouldn't be of much help and besides, we couldn't just stand there and wring our hands. I put Eva into a pan of hot water and she gradually relaxed and came out of it. Later, I learned that this was the best thing to do.

Curing fits was about my first doctoring in South Dakota, but not the last. When someone in the family got sick, I did what I remembered my mother doing. When we had colds, we slapped a cold pack on the chest. We used goose grease for sore muscles and swallowed sulphur and molasses to tone us up good in the spring. Somehow we survived the days when a doctor was ninety miles away in Pierre or even twenty-five miles away in Philip. Every family had some home remedies that may have helped, but of course, some people died every year because they couldn't get to a doctor in time. We homesteaders lived a hazardous existence.

I Go to Court

One morning in the summer of 1909, a man drove up to our place, tied his team, and knocked. When I opened the door, he handed me a piece of paper. I asked him what it was, and he said, "A subpoena to appear in court at 10 o'clock tomorrow in Ft. Pierre." I told him that my husband was already there defending a case about some hay he had sold, and I was all alone. "Who will take care of the children? Who will look after the livestock?", I said, "I can't go."

The man said that I had accepted the subpoena and therefore must appear, and whether I had problems getting some help or not was not his business. I saw that he had me. I thought for awhile and then asked him to put his team in the barn and feed them. He had driven twenty-five miles that morning and so the team needed feed and rest. While he looked after the children I would then go to the Hamptons and ask Essie if she could stay at our place for a day or two.

As I saddled a horse and showed him where the feed was kept, he told me why I was being called to appear in court. He said that the Claussens living about six miles beyond our place were having some real trouble. The mother had died of T.B. after they had moved out to Dakota, and the stepfather lived there on the claim with four step-children. The oldest girl was twenty years old and she was so crippled that she spent most of her time in a wheelchair. There was a boy of eighteen who had worked for us, and a girl of fifteen and one of eleven. The fifteen-year old girl wouldn't stay at home. When she could get a job she worked out, and when she wasn't working, she spent most of her time with the neighbors just working for her keep. For awhile, she stayed with a relative and went to school. To make a home for this sister, the boy declared himself the head of a family, filed on a homestead, and tried to get along by working around for the neighbors.

The girl came running to a neighbor one day, with tears in her eyes, saying that her stepfather had raped her. The woman examined her and saw that this was true, so it was reported to the county officials. Since the girl had been at our house often, they wanted me to go to court to testify. Shy had told the Claussen's lawyer that I would say in court that the girl was a liar and you couldn't believe a word that she said. Rape is a pretty serious charge so the lawyer was grasping for every straw to keep Claussen out of the penitentiary.

I rode over to the Hamptons and Essie got on behind me and we rode home. She took over inside and the deputy left for Philip. I got a team out of the pasture, harnessed them, and was on the way by mid-afternoon. It was good that I had washed the day before so I had enough diapers to take along for the baby. This was in the day before we fed babies out of bottles, but not before the railroad had reached Philip. I took the night train to Ft. Pierre and somehow managed to appear in court at 10 o'clock that morning. There I saw Shy for the first time since he had left home.

The Claussen lawyer took me into a small room and began questioning me. I was pretty much on the peck by this time, mad at Shy for telling Claussen that I would say in court that the girl was a liar and mad at the lawyer for his nasty attitude toward me. When he got through pumping at a dry well, he hadn't learned much from me except that I knew nothing about the girl and if called to the witness stand I would say absolutely nothing about her. He brought up the fact that my husband had given his word that I would testify but I told him that Shy could only speak for himself and that I would say that I knew nothing about the girl. He looked at me and said I looked like a pretty smart woman not to know anything. It was hard for me to understand why Claussen didn't plead guilty in the beginning.

I stayed four days but was never called on to testify that "I know nothing." The bailiff was good to me. My baby was hard to handle so I asked for some play things and a baby carriage, and the bailiff got them for me. The trial had gone to the jury before I left and later I learned that Claussen got twenty years in the penitentiary. He served only one year and managed to break out, and was never found. Here was one homesteader that we could afford to lose.

Shy Loses His Case

Everybody used the government land, or public domain, for pasturing livestock. There was no rent to pay or any planting to do. After a rancher used a certain range for awhile, he had the first rights there and nobody would move his stock in. When the homesteaders came, they built fences around their claims to keep cattle and sheep out, and this made it tough on livestock. The same thing was true for hay. Since the wild hay grew better on the low land than on high land, homesteaders cut their hay wherever they could find the best growth. This might be on the public domain or it might be on a claim that some homesteader had given up, or relinquished, as we said. It was this custom of cutting hay that got my husband in a real jam.

Shy had hired Leo Hagler to put up fifty tons of hay for him, enough to last our livestock all winter. Leo picked out the best places to mow, and stacked the hay just where he cut it, which was on the public domain. Then a settler named Griffith came along and homesteaded that piece of land. He dug into the middle of the hay stack and made a sort of a barn for his cow and two horses. When Shy went to haul the hay to our place to feed our livestock, Griffith wouldn't let him take all of it. He wanted enough to make a barn for his horses and cow but would let Shy take the rest of it. Really, I thought this pretty reasonable since the hay was on his land. But Shy had paid for putting up the hay and said he was going to take all of it. Griffith got his shotgun and ran Shy off of the claim.

We really needed the hay so we wrote to the attorney general in Pierre and asked him what to do. He told us "to replevy the hay" but in no case to start a law suit, and to give Griffith enough hay to last his livestock all winter. When Shy went to Midland to replevy the hay, he decided to start a suit anyway. This suit tied up the hay. When the case was called, Griffith had the case postponed. The winter wore on and the snow got deep. Since our cattle and horses were hungry, Shy had to scout around and buy hay at $10 a ton from the neighbors. In the meantime, the man had given the hay away to neighbors who had moved on claims next to him. When the trial was held, Griffith had his neighbors as witnesses and they claimed that part of the hay had been cut on their land. No doubt this was true since our hired man cut wherever he found the best hay. Of course, Shy lost the case and had to pay the court charges and expenses that ran up to $500. We didn't have the $500 so he mortgaged the livery stable he owned in Parker, where we had lived before moving west, and this mortgage was never paid off. When the mortgage was foreclosed later and Shy lost the stable, it was turned into a garage. Such is progress, but it is tough when the family had use for every cent we could get our hands on.

The hay lawsuit was just another example of Shy's not wanting to take advice from anyone, even the attorney general. It seems to me now that I was always cleaning up messes he made from just such bullheadedness.

Entertainment

In the early years when the homesteaders were scattered and none of them had more than a sod hut or a one or two-room log house, there wasn't much chance for the people to get together. But we had dances anyway at our house. Our house with two rooms was bigger than most settler's shacks, so we would move the bed and table outside and have a nice roomy space for dancing.

There was usually somebody around the country who could play a fiddle or accordion, and that was enough music with the stomp of the boots on the floor to help keep time. The young people coupled off and danced to their heart's content until morning, and many a romance started in this way. My young ones learned to dance before they learned to do much else. About everybody had babies but no baby-sitters so the children went everyplace with parents. They were put up in our attic and whether they slept or listened didn't matter. I danced very little since I was either carrying a baby or nursing one, and so I spent my time fixing the lunch or helping take care of other people's babies.

There was always a bottle of whiskey in most everyone's house, kept mostly for medicine for colds and snake bite. These bottles were brought to the dances and always someone drank more than he could hold. Some would try to straighten out old grudges. Frank Kurtzman once brought his little sweetheart to a dance and another settler's boy tried to take her away from him. With enough whiskey in him to make him brave, Frank pulled out his jack-knife and was going to cut the heart right out of this other fellow. We took the knife away from him, but the fight kept on. Frank scratched up the other fellow and I had to bind up the wounds. Frank sobered up fast when he saw blood. The other boy went home.

One time Sam Reber with his wife and four children, and his sister, Mae Stormer, started to our place for a dance. They lived near Powell and it was a long way to go. They were driving a democrat wagon. It was pitch dark and he missed the road leading off to our place. It was bitter cold and for the first time, he told us later, he didn't have a match to start a fire along the road. When they finally got to our place, the children were so cold their teeth chattered and the horses were worn out. Since the dance lasted until daylight, they still had a long time to visit with the other homesteaders and to dance all they wanted to.

As the country grew, so did the number of people who went to the dances. When we built a machine shed we started having dances out there. When the crowds outgrew our machine shed, we started having the parties in our new barn. The children loved to have dances in the loft. Since we had the mow filled with hay in the fall and winter, there wasn't much room for dancing until nearly spring and then only for a few months until we started filling it up with first cutting in July. In that time, we had a dance every other week. When the dance hall was built at Milesville, the neighborhood dances were held there.

Prohibition

When prohibition came along in 1920, the bootlegger peddled booze to anybody who wanted it and some of the people started making home-brew on their own. We quit having dances in the barn since we were afraid that some careless smoker might set fire to the hay. Besides, quite a lot of the young boys drank too much.

Shy never cared anything about liquor and opposed its use by anybody. But our young sprouts made some home-brew right under his nose without him knowing it. They thought it was fun to make their own beer. Using a recipe they had heard about, they took a ten-gallon jar from our basement, hid it where they thought I wouldn't find it in the hay, and proceeded to mix up a mess of home-brew. I never let on that I knew about it, but about the time it was ready to bottle, I emptied a pound of Epsom salts into it.

One night they invited some of their friends over to try their concoction. When they came out of the barn, they were a bunch of pretty sick pups. They must have decided to get out of business right then, for they ditched their beer and never once said anything to me about how they got so sick.

Ivar Johnson, a bachelor living up the stream on a claim, felt sorry for the boys, and said to Jasper, "Your mother has lots of pieplant. You bring me some and I will make you some wine." When I discovered they had pulled my rhubarb, I asked them what they had done with it. They didn't want to get Ivar involved and so wouldn't tell me anything. So I took the car and tracked them, first over to the old Sichterman house, and then down toward Ivar's place, and there I lost the tracks. In the meantime, one of the boys had got on his horse and ridden over to Ivar's and told him that I was on the trail of the pieplant. Ivar said, "Oh, my God, I don't want her on my neck, boys. Let's ditch the wine and forget all about it." With that, the idea of making beer or wine seemed to have died a natural death.

CHAPTER IX

Expanding the Homestead, and Taking Root

A Swedish homesteader took a claim on the South Dakota-Nebraska border, but was uncertain in which state he lived. When he got a surveyor and learned he lived in Nebraska, he threw his hat in the air, shouted: "No more of them awful South Dakota winters."

Land, Taxes, and Tax Deeds

Homesteading west of the missouri was a hazardous business. It was a country really made for livestock instead of grain farming. But we settlers had only 160 acres in the early years and that is not enough land to support many critters or to make a living raising cash crops. We had to increase our holdings or get out. A lot of our neighbors sold their relinquishment, or claim to a homestead, and moved on somewhere. Some of the homesteads were taken up by people who didn't expect to settle there, but were there only to make a little money. The families that didn't know much about dry farming failed. In a way, we managed to stay by buying up the land of the people who couldn't make it.

It was 1907 when I got my first lesson on paying taxes. I was visiting our neighbors, the Stephensons, and was sitting in their outhouse reading our county newspaper. The name of S. B. Fairchild caught my eye. I read the item that said that our homestead had been sold for back taxes, and that a man in Ft. Pierre had bought it up. I went home and asked Shy if he had paid the taxes. He said, "What taxes? You don't have to pay taxes on a homestead. It's free." From that time on, I decided that I had to pay the taxes myself and take over the running of the place. It took a lot of money to clear up the title to our 160 acres and the personal property we had on it. After that, I kept track of our taxes and the sales of land for unpaid taxes.

Sometimes it was pretty hard to meet taxes when they came due. We were setting up a new county and new townships, building roads and all of this cost money. If there is anything a homesteader doesn't have much of, it is ready cash. He may have livestock and even title to his land, but he can't pay taxes with cows and deeds. Taxes were too high when it came to what the land brought in.

Drought and Depressions

In the drought year of 1911, the homesteaders organized two townships into one and floated $10,000 worth of bonds, half going to Top Bar Township 5 and half to Marietta Township 6. The money was used for relief and was to be worked out on the roads. At this time, Shy was down in the Nebraska Sand Hills where the grass was better, with the cattle and horses. When the town board was giving out the money, they decided that the Fairchilds were not entitled to it. They made the excuse that I had no one at the place to work out my $50 on the road. I guess they really believed that we were better off than most of them. We were, in that we had more livestock than most of them, but that wasn't cash for paying taxes and buying some things to eat. Everybody was poor, except in land and livestock.

I told the town board that I wanted the $50 since I would have to help pay back the bonds when they came due, and that I wanted my part of the road work done right near our place. I would see that the work was done right. I hired a man to do the work on the road, but they sent him home saying that if I couldn't do any of the work I wouldn't get the $50. The hired man was a contrary cuss and so he just sat there until they finally let him go to work. It took the township years and years to pay off the bonds. The town had paid a broker $500 just for selling the bonds and also paid a high rate of interest. By the time the debt was paid up, the township had paid out $15,000 on the $10,000 which it had borrowed. A drought year is hard to live through, but most any year was hard on homesteaders.

A lot of homesteaders left the country in 1911 when the

drought dried up the pastures and killed most of the crops. Those of us who stayed used all the land that had been left behind. We cut hay on the low land and harvested anything we could find. In the years after 1911, we got enough crops from these abandoned claims to pay up the back taxes and get clear titles to the land.

When the next land boom came along in 1917, because of World War I, another bunch of settlers came in. Many of them sold their holdings back East and paid high prices for land west of the Missouri. My Uncle Allen Horsfall was one of them. He bought a sizable piece northeast of Philip, paying $25 an acre, and mortgaging for the unpaid balance. He improved it and put a renter on it. When the price of wheat collapsed after World War I, he lost the place. It was the same with a lot of others. For a second time, the settlers moved out, losing everything. The old die-hards among us stayed on and used the vacated land just as we had done before. It was next to impossible for an absentee owner to collect any rent. It just wasn't worth the effort. Some of us picked up land for back taxes.

Then in the 1930's we had another depression. Not only were prices low, but our range dried up because of the drought and grasshoppers ate up everything that was left. Up to about 1930, we hadn't been eaten up with anything except grasshoppers and cut-worms. About this time, gray beetles showed up and took over the gardens and shrubs. We knocked them off the plants into a pan of kerosene. In 1935 we didn't even have cut worms since there wasn't anything for them to eat. I guess they just starved to death that year. We had some rain in 1935, but in 1936 both grasshoppers and beetles showed up again. For the next few years we had some rain but we also had hordes of grasshoppers, and they took everything. Unless a person has lived through a grasshopper invasion, he can't understand what a terrible thing it is to look out and see them swarming by the millions and when they land, they take everything. When I say everything, I mean just that, for they take not only the crops, but also the leaves and the bark from the trees. They even ate the curtains and our clothing. By 1940, the grasshopper days seemed to be on the way out. Poisons were being used on them even if it was dangerous to livestock. I guess they come and go in cycles, and they usually came when drought had us against the wall anyway.

Buying Land

As has been said, the Fairchild clan had its beginning west of the Missouri in 1901. Shy and his son, Fred, had left Parker after the crops were in that fall and headed for Chamberlain on the Missouri River. Traveling in a buggy pulled by a good team, and leading a saddle horse, they looked at the country around Chamberlain but didn't find any free land to their liking. Shy sent me a telegram asking me to send him a tarp, a saddle, and some bedding and said they were going on west. They drove past Murdo and on toward the Cheyenne River. They found a piece of land that they liked north of the present Milesville. It had a nice spring on it but they learned that it was already filed on by someone. This man wasn't too interested in it and his wife was ready to move on, but he got cold feet when it came to selling his "relinquishment" rights. The cattlemen around there heard that this man was going to sell to a sheepman and they didn't think sheepmen were good enough citizens for that part of South Dakota. Shy and Fred moved on, found the Lindsay place for sale, and Fred bought it with Shy's help.

Lindsay had filed on the land but had not proved up on it. He had built a shack, made an ice house in the hill, and dug a cave for keeping vegetables. Shy and Fred paid him $500 for his relinquishment and improvements - a twelve by twenty-four foot cabin, a few chickens, and even the household goods. It seems that Lindsay had left a few days before they came along. Earlier, leaving his wife to hold down the place, he had fenced in some good waterholes on his place that range cattle had been using for a good long time and so the word was around that something might happen to him. It was said that he had put his brand on some cows or calves he didn't own. Anyway, he got scared and left the country as fast as he could ride out of it. Mrs. Lindsay was glad to sell out everything they owned and to get out without any more trouble.

In October, 1901, Fred married Eleanor Stobbs, and set out for the Lindsay claim. They lived there for the remaining eighteen months required for proving up. Later they learned that the land they had filed on was not the Lindsay land, but was really the piece adjoining where they lived. They did not discover the mistake until Warren Rogers filed on what they thought was the Lindsay land. Since a husband and wife cannot both prove up on a claim at the same time, Eleanor filed on this quarter section and later Fred filed on a piece in the Spotted Bear breaks to the north.

Shy had filed his claim on the little creek when he was out in the fall of 1901. When Fred and Eleanor left the quarter section a mile and a quarter west of our place and the Spotted Bear piece, Shy bought them out. This gave us three quarter sections.

My mother homesteaded across the creek from us to the southeast in Section 33, Township 5, Range 20, and lived there alone while she proved up her claim. Then we bought her land for $1,000 and agreed to pay her $100 a year. When we had her paid, we got the deed, and this gave us four quarter sections.

90

Shy's sister, Lucy Morris, a widow, came out in 1906 and filed on a piece of land lying next to our place on the east. She promised to sell it to us when she got proved up on it. We built her log house about three rods from ours and kept her in groceries and fuel while she was living there. She paid the proving up cost of the land which was $80. When she got her patent from the government we were to give her $300 and get a deed for it. But she changed her mind and deeded the land to her daughter, Birdie Maupin.

My mother was on her claim at this time. One day both mother and Lucy were at our house. Lucy picked up little Leah and said to her, "You poor little thing. God took one of your little ribs and made some boy." Mother came back fast. "For Heaven sakes, Lucy, you don't believe that, do you?" Lucy fell on her knees and beseeched God to strike her dead if she ever failed to abide by His Holy Word. My mother thought she had gone crazy. All of this didn't surprise me since I had heard her talk this way before. She had never been very well organized. When she got off the stage at our place in 1906, it was a total surprise for we didn't know that she was even thinking about coming out to get some free land. But she had read in the papers about South Dakota and just decided to come out and get a homestead and then sell it. She made it clear that she wanted money for her land and wanted her own price of $300. We agreed to pay it, but it wasn't until 1949 that I got title to this quarter section and then I got it for back taxes.

In the depression of the 1930's, land values went down to nothing. The county held a sizeable part of this land for back taxes. After four years of delinquency, the county could put the property up for sale to the highest bidder. The county could then give a tax title deed to the buyer who could get the title cleared. When the New Deal conservation programs came along, people who stayed in Dakota got interested in picking up tax titles. When World War II came along in 1941 with high prices, the farmers were all set to make some money raising wheat and livestock.

By the time I bought Lucy Morris' land in 1949, I had put together 1440 acres and had my roots pretty deep in South Dakota soil.

Fred Fairchild

After we bought Eleanor's claim, Fred moved over on the Spotted Bear place and began to run sheep. We used the little Lindsay cabin for our first school house and later moved it over close to our place. Fred got a bunch of sheep from E. A. Morrison on the shares, and they spread out on that range. He was not a rancher,

91

but liked to read and talk all day about socialism and atheism. Sheep herding suffers when the man in charge spends his time doing other things. In time, he managed somehow to build a nice home, a big shed, and a dam that backed up a lot of water, but the sheep business never got along very well.

We used to see Fred and his family at Christmas or Thanksgiving but the children visited back and forth more often. I liked his wife, Eleanor, but never knew why in the hell they built their house right down in a gulch that was as hard to get to as a robbers' roost. One time when we were there, Fred said to me, "Grace, I wish you would keep your kids home so my kids wouldn't want to go so much." I told him that I had enough trouble of my own without taking on any more.

School Land

A man named Beadle had got the legislature to pass a law setting aside two sections in each township as a school fund. The rent and income from sale of this land was to go into the fund, and no land was to be sold for less than $10 an acre. This brought in a sizable sum of money which was allotted to each county for making loans. Stanley County was one of the borrowers, and helped the settlers get out from under the high interest rates charged by the banks. Later, General Beadle State College was named after him.

When the depression years came along, the state was left holding the bag in many cases. To meet the deficit, the rural credit commission was set up and the state was bonded for several million dollars. The debt seemed to be small at the time but as the depression stretched out and people could not pay back what they had borrowed, the state had to borrow more and more to meet the deficit. Schools have always been hard to support west of the Missouri. It was made more difficult by the people who never cared whether school kept on or not.

The Nebraska Sand Hills

In the early years we always had hope that things might get better, but in the drought and depression years we doubted if this could happen. Congress had passed a new Homestead Act allowing anyone who had taken up 160 acres before to add three more quarter sections from the public domain, making a total of 640 acres. The quarter sections did not have to be next to each other. When the drought of 1911 came, Shy heard that the Sand Hills of northern Nebraska were covered with green grass and so he decided to go down there, taking the livestock with him, and stake out another piece of land.

Expanding the Homestead, and Taking Root

At this time, young Leo Hagler was working for us. He had come out to Dakota when he was seventeen. His mother, a Civil War widow, with a $12 a month pension, filed on a claim over on the Cheyenne River. Leo was a good dependable boy and now that he was twenty-one he was also interested in getting a piece of land. The Sand Hills of Nebraska looked good to him, too. He and Shy drove our cattle down there in the fall of 1911 and spent the winter there. I went down the next spring to look over the country. Shy and Leo filed on land but I couldn't see that it would help us much to move. It was bunch grass country about like it was where we lived. There were lots of cattle and horses there but not many settlers had taken up homesteads. There were no schools except the Indian schools, and I felt that we just had to give our children an education. When I thought of moving, I couldn't think of anything to take with us. Our cattle were mort-gaged and could not be moved out of Dakota. I knew that we had to have more land to get along where we were, but we did have a school started and we did have neighbors around. Why drag the children into another wilderness and start all over again? I said, no, we would stay in South Dakota.

Shy would bring up the subject every now and then. He was always footloose and ready to find heaven on earth somewhere else. When World War I came along and land prices boomed, he talked about moving to the Sand Hills again. Will Walpole, a land agent, came to our place one day and offered us $25 an acre for our land. Shy was ready to sell. He seemed to skirt around the main problem: What would we do with the children after we got them there? I said, "no, we're going to see this through right where we are." That ended that.

> There was a homesteader from Quebec,
> Who was buried in snow up to his neck;
> When asked, "Are you friz?"
> He replied, "Yes, I is,
> Cause snow's not this deep in Quebec."

Adapted from A. B. Gilfillan, *Sheep*
(U. of Minn. Press, 1957), p. 83.

The family poses in front of the old house

CHAPTER X

Building a Home and Buying Tractors

*"It was so cold that I saw two jack rabbits
pushing a cottontail to get him started."*

*"We had eleven months of winter
and one month of poor sledding."*

From Carts and Surrey to Mountain Buggy

When Shy loaded the emigrant car in Parker, South Dakota, in the spring of 1902, he took care of first things first, as he saw it, and put in two racing carts and a wagon. One of the carts was a sulky and the other was a breaking cart. Both of them were nuisances and didn't have much use on a Dakota homestead. But Shy's dream of a life west of the Missouri was that of running a horse ranch. He wasn't much concerned with raising corn and stacking hay so the animals could live through the winter. Somehow, carts didn't do us much good in getting places and the wagon was good only for hauling lumber and heavy things. We needed a carriage or a surrey.

We sent to Elkhart, Indiana, for a surrey, and when it came, it was a nifty affair with a fringe around the top and with side curtains. Such a beautiful thing couldn't be left out in the weather, so we built a machine shed and carriage house south of the house. This shed was twenty-four by twenty-four feet and was an eye sore to me because it cut off our view of the little creek. When we put a floor in it, it made a good dance hall, especially when my organ helped supply the music. My mother had bought an Estey organ when I was ten years old, and when she broke up housekeeping the year I married Shy, she gave it to me. It was the only touch of elegance that we had on our ranch and I loved it for what it was, something beyond just making a living.

Life could be drab there on the claim. I tried to brighten it up with flowers and trees. On the north side of the machine shed we planted three cottonwood trees, protecting them with woven wire. That was also where I put my pansies and sweet peas. When the cottonwoods got about ten inches in size, we had a warm spell in February, they budded out, then came a cold wave, and they died.

While Shy was buying cattle from Corb Morse, Corb used what he called a mountain buggy to take Shy around to see them. It wasn't long until Shy had traded the surrey for one of the mountain buggies. None of us was very happy about the trade. The surrey had been roomier, had a top, and was more comfortable. The mountain buggy was more like a wagon, It had only one seat so when I used it, I had to put the children under the seat and in front of my feet.

Sheds and Barns

Our first shelter for the stock was a hay-covered shed. After a few years, the roof began to leak and the cattle wallowed knee-deep in mud and manure. It was solid in the winter but in the spring, when it began to thaw, it got to be a terrible mess. A cow even got stuck in the mire once and had to be pulled out with a team.

It was the children's job to take care of the livestock when they got old enough to do it. They had to wade around in the muck to feed them. They got manure and mud on their clothes and packed it into the house on their shoes. Flies hung around both the shed and the house in swarms. Pet colts, pet pigs, and pet calves poked holes in the screen door and flies poured in. They were in the milk, on the butter, and in the sugar. We shooed them out so we could eat without having to swat flies all the time. We certainly had to get rid of them and that meant tearing down the old shed.

We needed a new barn of some kind. By this time we had a steady income from cream and butter but we lacked a clean place to do our milking in. Shy's insurance policy with Modern Wood-

96

man was about paid up and it was worth $665. It looked as if we might swing a new barn. We drew up the plans, got estimates from the Sterns Bros. Mill in Rapid City, and found that we could build a barn forty-six by fifty-six feet, with a round roof and a concrete retaining wall on the northwest slope, all for $600, using the Black Hills lumber instead of pine from Minnesota and Wisconsin.

We asked the insurance company to cancel out Shy's policy, and they sent the check to the insurance clerk in Philip, and he handed it over to Shy. We still owed $600 on our cattle so my husband marched down to the bank and paid off that mortgage, and proudly brought home the cancelled note. He forgot all about the new barn. "What about the barn," I shouted at him, "From this day on, I am not making the children wade around in that filthy barnyard to milk the cows. If there is any milking to be done, you'll do it." Shy did not like to milk, so when faced with the wrath of a woman, he went to Philip and bought enough lumber to build a little barn eighteen by twenty-four feet. We still had to use the old shed. Besides, Shy built the new barn in the little draw only sixty feet from the house. When the water came up the draw it flowed through the barn. During one down-pour, we heard the calves bawling and knocking around in the barn. Shy hurried out. The barn was full of water. He managed to get up in the mow and when the little calves swam past the hay hole, he would grab a calf by the leg and pull it up.

I told the boys to pull down a part of the old shed, dig into the hill, and get ready for a new barn. I had had enough of flies and floods and manure. Shy got into the spirit of the thing and hauled sand day after day. We got Ed Stephenson to help with the cement foundation, and so we finally got our new barn under way. Jasper took the plans to Rapid City. One of the neighbors wanted some lumber so with his order and our order, we bought a carload and got a good price. The little barn in the draw was torn down and the lumber used in the new barn. A carpenter with the help of the boys put up the barn. Were we ever proud when the last nail was driven and we had a NEW BARN! Our place really looked showy with this new building, a nice woven wire fence, and shrubbery around the yard.

The Kitchen

I had been hoping to get the kitchen made over for a long time, but never got very far. Jasper was nearly fifteen and after helping on the barn, he thought he was quite a carpenter. "Mamma," he said, "if you will tell me what you want done, I will do it for you." It was time to start on the house. We moved the chimney from the middle of the room to the side of the house, then changed the stairway, built in cupboards, and made much more room. Neither Jasper nor I had ever laid up any brick chimneys and we had our troubles. When we put the cement on, it would dry before we could lay on the next brick. We finally figured out that the bricks were so dry that they were soaking up the moisture out of the cement, so we soaked our bricks and got our chimney up. It is still in good shape today. What a change in not having to look at ten lengths of stove pipe in the kitchen!

We had quite a problem in making our stairway. I didn't want it to take much space and I wanted it enclosed, so we decided on a winding stair. I laid out paste-board pieces to show Jasper what it looked like since he had never seen one. We made one step at a time and got a pretty good stairway out of it and even had a little closet underneath. After we had it all done and visitors would look at it and tell us how much better the house looked, Shy would puff up like a toad and say, "Yes, it's a lot better than it was before and it sure was a lot of work." That was a pretty strong boast for a man who had never lifted his hands to help.

In order to protect the logs in the walls, Shy had built a porch four and a half feet wide all around the house except on the west end where we had added the room. He had expected to keep the rain out of the house, but it never worked. We finally tore off this porch, put paper and siding over the logs and this kept the floor dry inside.

The dirt cellar under part of the house kept causing us trouble by caving in every now and then. I decided to do something about it. The cellar door that was in the living room was dangerous, for a person could walk in through the front door and fall into the cellar hole. I wanted to move the door. Shy said, "Why not put in some posts and nail slats across them to hold back the dirt?" When I objected, he stomped out of the house, saying, "Do it your way. I wash my hands of the whole thing." So I put in a cement basement under the house, with the help of the boys.

To make the old log house a little more livable, I had to find the money myself. The bank was taking any income the farm produced to pay on the mortgage. I decided to raise chickens. I had had a few hens for some time to have eggs and a few fried chickens in the summer. Now I would go at it in a bigger way. When the old hens began to want to set in latter February, I had the eggs ready for them. There wasn't any hen house so I set the hens in boxes around in the house, in the bedrooms, under the table, in the bureau drawers, wherever I could find a place to put them. Every day I took the hens out to the pen, fed and watered them, and brought them back to their nests. I had chickens ready for the early market, and got a good price. That fall I built myself a good chicken house, and went at the chicken business in a bigger way the next year. I partitioned off one part for setting hens and baby chicks, and began to think of a new basement under the whole house.

One day I went over to a neighbors and when I got back, I had some real trouble on my hands. An old sow had got out of her pen, eaten 102 chickens and turned up all the nests. Shy had turned the old sow out to get some exercise and while she ate chickens, he slept. I had to begin all over again if I was to get my basement.

By fall, I thought I had enough chicken and egg money to put the basement in. I saw a mason and he agreed to put it in for $90 if I furnished the cement — and the hole. I hired a man to dig the hole deeper and to straighten out the walls, and I wheeled out the dirt in a wheelbarrow myself. When the mason, Fred Haberly, got there, everything was ready for him. He did a good job and it has been a pleasure ever since having a storeroom for canned goods, fruits and vegetables, and it was a cool place for milk and butter when we didn't have ice.

By this time, the house was getting pretty crowded with our family. We needed to add some rooms. I got an estimate on the cost of adding an entry room on the south side and two bedrooms ten by twenty feet on the north side of the house. The lumber and labor would cost $400, if we could give the carpenter some help. But I couldn't swing it that year. My chickens brought in only $300. I told this to the lumberman and he said, "If you want these rooms, go ahead and build them and pay me when you can." So I did just that. One bedroom we gave over to Mildred and the room off the kitchen was for the boys and when they were not there I used it as a sewing room. We had enclosed part of the old porch earlier and this became a part of the kitchen, which enlarged it into a kitchen-dining room combined.

The flies in the fall were always bad, and they seemed to hang around the south door. So I decided to put on a shed twelve by twenty feet on the south side of the house. It was very low, and when my son-in-law who is six feet two came to visit us, he had to duck to get into the house.

When we had bought brick for the chimney we had some left over. Why not build a cistern next to the west door and run the pipe into the kitchen so we could have soft water at any time.? We hired two men to dig the hole, eight by ten feet. Breemes, who worked on top, was overly religious while Johnson, who worked at the bottom, was the opposite. Breemes thought he could convert Johnson, but when Johnson didn't see the light, they would get in a hot argument. I was afraid that Breemes would drop a bucket of dirt on Johnson to make him see the true way. I asked Shy to help out but he didn't get along any better. Finally, we hired two different men to get the hole dug without religious problems. Charlie Motch laid the bricks for the cistern and he must have done a good job since it holds water to this day. It seemed wonderful to have soft water, but to have both hard and soft was nothing short of a miracle in that country. Nearly all the wells west of the Missouri are very hard, and water coming from an alkali bed is pretty common. Anybody who drinks such water and isn't accustomed to it will get as sick as a poisoned pup.

Buying a Tractor

The boys were growing up fast. All the work on the ranch had been done with horses of which we always had an over-supply. The boys were getting tired of cleaning out the barn after the two four-horse teams every day and hitching them up, having runaways and breaking up machinery. In the summer flies bothered the horses even if flynets were used. The nets were always getting torn up and needing mending. Tractors were appearing here and there, but were not in general use.

For some time I had talked about swapping some of the extra horses for a tractor, but Shy always refused to go along. One day when I was in the blacksmith shop, I heard John Urban talking about a tractor he had. He wasn't very well and the help he had expected to have to run it had left and he would sell it at cost if the buyer would take over the work he had contracted to do. The price, he said, was $750 for the tractor, tandem disc, plow, and drag. When I heard this, I thought it was just what we had been waiting for.

I came home and talked the matter over with the family. They all were for buying the tractor except Shy. He just knew that it wouldn't work. No cash was needed for the first payment since that would come out of the contract jobs. Well, the long and short of it was, we bought the tractor, a Titan. We used it for four years without spending a cent on it for repairs. We broke a lot of tough prairie with it. The boys were young and didn't know anything about machinery, but they made the shift from horse to tractor without much trouble. Shy wouldn't touch it. I don't think he ever sat on the seat or put his hand on the wheel. He was like the old farmer who saw an elephant for the first time, and said, "There ain't no such animal."

The Titan did a lot more work than the horses and cut down on the flies around the barn and house and it worked like its name - a giant. One day it almost buried itself when it dropped into a quagmire on the side of a hill. Before Joe knew what was happen-

100

ing the hind wheels were in mud up to the hub and the front wheels were on dry ground. It took big posts, planks, and a four-horse team with a block and tackle to pull that tractor out of the mire. There must have been a flow of water below there that hit a sand pocket and had nearly reached the top of the ground at that point. Strange as it may seem, when we had our droughts in 1934 and 1936, we never thought to dig into that spot for water.

The old Titan needed some repairs when we got ready for the fifth year. We had bought the parts, but before we had them installed a salesman for Rumley tractors came along. We visited awhile and he went away without a sale as we told him that we weren't in the market for such a big tractor. About a week later the Rumley agent drove into the yard and took Shy for a ride. When they came back, my husband had bought a Rumley for $2,000. We were all disgusted beyond words. The Titan was included in the deal and notes were signed providing for payments for several years. We were face to face with the old mortgage again.

This was the straw that broke the camel's back. The tractor Shy had bought had been a demonstrator and had been lying around for a couple of years. It was not long on the job. The water pump didn't work. We couldn't get a man out to repair it for six weeks, and then he found a cracked sleeve and other problems. It was two months before it was working again. All spring work had been at a standstill. The first note was due and so money due the bank had to be put on the Rumley debt. The older boys went to work to earn money for their schooling and the younger ones carried on. I had had just about as much of this as I could take.

Buying the Dodge

Shy sort of thought he would like to move to the Black Hills, but he didn't have anything lined up. I couldn't see any reason for moving unless he found a gold mine, and so I refused to sign my name to the deed for the sale of the land. I held this as a whip over him for a good many years. In 1917, while prices were high, we had an auction and sold off some of our extra horses. The government was buying them for the cavalry and prices were good. We sold thirty head for an average of $50 apiece. We also sold around thirty-five head of cattle, leaving us just fifteen milk cows and a bull. The money from this sale paid off our debt to the First National Bank of Pierre and left us $63 in cash to the good. We were as happy as could be, for this was the first time in our whole married life that we weren't in debt. This freedom from debt lasted just two weeks!

When Fred came over to take his father into Philip in his Model

Frontier Woman

T, I should have known that something would happen. Emma was in her third year of high school there. That was the year of the big "flu" epidemic and she had been driving a car for Dr. Gearhart, going day and night to look after people. She got paid $5 a day, and no doubt was enthusiastic about automobiles. Whether she had anything to do with it, I don't know, but that same evening she came home with Shy in a new Dodge car, both as happy as clams.

When I saw them pull up, my heart fell, and my temperature went up. "My God, what has he done now," I thought. I did not even go out of the house to look at the car, but the children ran out and flocked around to admire this new contraption. Shy stood as proud as a rooster and told the kids that he had bought it so they would stay home on the ranch. What a farce! When he came into the house, I asked what it cost. He proudly said, "$1,070." I then asked how he had paid for it, and he proudly said he had paid cash. "Where did you get the cash?" I asked. "Why, at the bank, of course. I mortgaged the cattle so we could have a new car."

Here we were working for the bank again. If I could have flown the coop, without leaving a bunch of kids behind, I would have done it right then. The children were in school and we needed a lot of money. I was dead set on getting them an education. It took a lot of money to run the car. After awhile we borrowed money from the school district at five percent and paid off the bank note which carried ten percent. Our cattle were free again but now the land carried the mortgage.

CHAPTER XI

Farming the Dry Country

Fifty miles from water,
A hundred miles to wood,
To hell with this damned country,
I'm going home for good.

"Textbook Farming"

Old Stanley Country comprised everything west of the Missouri in South Dakota between the Cheyenne River on the north and west and the White River on the south, a country of 4,146 square miles lodged in between Indian reservations on the south and on the north. It was a great grass empire where thousands of cattle and horses had roamed for years before we homesteaders took it over. After we got through the early years and the droughts and depressions had frozen out many of the pioneers, we learned that to survive a rancher needed to raise both livestock and crops that would grow in a region where there wasn't much rainfall. Most little ranchers looked down their noses at any kind of "textbook farming," but to me it was the only way to adapt to a dry country. The State College at Brookings was to be a great help to all of us who believed in trying new things.

When the County Superintendent of Schools, W. W. Werner, visited our school in 1912, he stayed all night at our house. Jasper

103

was just ten years old, and that is why Mr. Werner wanted to talk to us about 4-H Club work for him. He was in charge of getting it started in Stanley County and wanted us to help set up a club that would try new crops and strains of livestock. He hoped that some of this new "textbook farming" would rub off on the settlers.

Jasper was enrolled as a 4-H Club member and in time his club book came; and though Shy had no interest in "textbook farming," I did, and so I sent for several bulletins from the Extension Service at Brookings. Mr. Werner hadn't been able to get other boys to sign up, so Jasper was the only one. Little did he know how much depended on him to help us survive in that country! In time, Jasper received six pounds of Yellow Dent corn seed, a new variety that had been developed in North Dakota. Jasper, with the help of his dad, plowed, harrowed, and planted a piece of ground, and cared for the Yellow Dent corn all summer long. That fall, a sample was sent to the exhibit at Ft. Pierre, along with his work book. I don't recall that he got any prize, but I do know that the 4-H Club corn plot opened up doors for all of us. Our other boys joined the Club as they came along and so we were always trying new seeds that the experimental stations were developing for the dry plains. It was a sad and rare day when one of the boys didn't bring home some prize from the State Fair.

During the first visit with Mr. Werner, he talked about alfalfa, a new crop in that country. It had been grown back in Wisconsin, and also in the Black Hills of South Dakota under irrigation. There were also a few experimental plots along the Cheyenne River north of our place. Charlie Haxby was raising it for feed and seed. Shy had been over to Haxby's and fed some of the alfalfa to his horses, but said they didn't like it as well as grass and so he decided that it was not fit feed for horses. I was anxious to get some started on our place, but he would not let me plant any. Before Werner left that day, I asked him if he would send me some seed anyway and he said he would be glad to send a few pounds. "Maybe," he said, "you can talk your husband into planting it for you."

I had to keep that alfalfa seed two years before I ever got it into the ground. The hired hand had heard me pleading for a little piece of land to plant the seed and had heard Shy turn me down, saying that he didn't want "to get that weed started on the place." There was a little piece of land ready for oats, so the hired hand said to me on the sly, "If you want me to plant the alfalfa in with the oats, I'll do it for you." It was a good feeling to know that at last we had the seed in the ground even if it was two years old and had been done behind Shy's back. It wasn't long until we had a swell stand of alfalfa with a few oats scattered in it.

Farming the Dry Country

When Shy discovered that he had been tricked, he was as mad as a wet hen. It gnawed at him all summer long. The next spring he hitched his team to the plow and plowed it all under, and thought he had rid the place of this "weed." But he did not kill it out. The plowing made it a better patch. We cut it once for hay and then let it go for seed, and got a bushel and a peck from that little patch. The horses and cattle ate it and got fat off of it. After that, Shy was sold on alfalfa hay. From that little beginning we seeded over 200 acres and put up hundreds of tons of feed until the drought of the 1930's killed it off. Grasshoppers and beetles made it almost impossible to grow alfalfa until 1948 when a few people got it started again.

4-H Clubs

By 1917 Stanley County was divided into three smaller counties — Jackson, Haakon, and Stanley. Haakon County, in which we now live, hired Freda Morrison as our first Assistant County Agent. She carried on the 4-H Club work and gave home demonstrations. By that time we had several 4-H Clubs in the county and our children were exhibiting their work at the county fair. Joe Morrison was Project Leader one year, and his enthusiasm had the boys excited about trying new things. He gave each boy one bushel of a new kind of soft wheat that had been developed at the State College Experimental Farm. It was a macaroni wheat and it did very well. From these beginnings, we started raising it, and so did the neighbors. We quit growing it when the elevators began to spring up around the country and wheat was shipped out to Minneapolis and other places for milling.

The corn that Jasper grew on his 4-H plot proved adaptable to our land. It was early and the stock liked it, and it was used for many years as a standard seed corn. Later on, a variety of white corn along with varieties of squaw corn were tried out on the boys' plots, and some of these proved to be adaptable to the country. These experiments gave us the edge on many homesteaders since many of them brought out seed from Iowa and Illinois and other states to the east, and found that their crops failed. We learned to make farming pay by planting seeds developed for that dry country west of the Missouri.

One year Byron decided to try a different crop, flax, on his 4-H plot. It was new out there with us and didn't turn out so well. When he mowed it, the mower sickle gummed up. He would wash the sickle and try again, only to have the same thing happen. Then he would clean it with kerosene, try again, bawl awhile, clean it off, and try again. Finally, he came into the house, looked at me grimly, and said, "I'm not going to do anything more with that flax, and no amount of argument from you or anybody else is going to make me." So we turned the stock into the plot and boy, did they ever have lovely coats that fall!

Professor Hansen

For almost ten years after 1929 we were without crops and trying to keep our heads above water on the old homestead. Our alfalfa was gone and most of the feed crops dried up or were eaten by grasshoppers and beetles. It looked as if the whole country west of the Missouri was going to blow away. A lot of the homesteaders who had survived over the years gave up and headed back east. I had read a good deal about crested wheat grass in the farm bulletins and got interested in it. It had been brought from Siberia by Professor Hansen of South Dakota State, and when he visited us his stories about it whetted my appetite for trying it. When the New Deal came along in the 1930's, our chance came to try this new grass. In the new farm program we were asked to lay by some of the land and not use it for wheat. To earn the payments allotted us for this, I seeded sixty acres to crested wheat grass. The first year it looked as if it was a good thing. The second year, I had a good seed crop but like many other new-fangled things in the experimental stage, crested wheat as a feed crop was a flop. It seemed to starve the soil and it rootbound itself so that it didn't get very high. Besides, its nutritious value as a feed was small. We were stung with bumpy fields to mow and got only a good pasture for early spring and late fall. In time, it starved itself out. It never did us much good, though it did help keep the tops of gulleys from blowing away and did stop some erosion that was prevalent in the rough country.

Professor Hansen visited our place several times and talked about his experiments. I remembered my childhood days roaming the hills of southern Wisconsin and the nursery stock my father used to bring home to set out. When Professor Hansen wanted me to help with his experiments for getting new plants for the dry country, I was much interested and wanted to help. We worked together on a new berry, a cross between a sand cherry and a choke cherry. I would find the nicest choke cherries, just as I had done as a little girl, and send him cuttings. He would send me many of his plants and I would try them out in our country. These things kept me from just sitting and rotting on our homestead when the going was tough. There were always things to do and to learn, and I find that as true today as it was years ago.

I couldn't see any reason why land which would produce such good grain wouldn't be good for other things such as were grown

106

in the eastern part of South Dakota. Of course, we didn't have water, but that didn't seem to be a problem that couldn't be solved by experimenting with different shrubs and seeds. As the years went by, I found that we could grow most anything adapted to this country, except in the drought years. The settlers who talked down "textbook farming" either got out of the country or turned to other means of making a living.

The country west of the Missouri was covered with a native grass called gama grass by Professor Hansen but bunch grass by the stockmen who used it for a pasture. Actually, there were several gama grasses. We called one of them buffalo grass, another nigger wool, and a tall one we just called wheat grass. Nigger grass was the devil itself to plow up. Its roots were so thick and so deep that they would stay in lumps for years. A harrow with its sharp tines wouldn't break up a clump. The wheat grass was very good feed. We cut it for the livestock in the drought years and sold some of the hay to neighbors. The government offered to buy buffalo grass seed, so we harvested it with special machinery and sold it for reseeding the dust bowl where grasses had disappeared from too much grazing or where wheat farmers had plowed up land that should have been kept as range.

After we had worked with the State College people for a few years, I got interested in knowing what kind of soil we had on our place, and decided to have it tested. I took samples from several areas on the ten acre piece east of the house and sent them to the laboratory at State College. I found that there were seven different kinds of soil, each with different elements in them. Some of it was straight gumbo where nothing would grow. Then there were sandy spots, heavy black loam, and other types. The gumbo would produce good crops if we put a lot of fertilizer on it, but without manure, it just grew a little weed that was sour tasting but which the sheep were crazy to eat. We called this salt weed. The cattle would eat the weed and lick the ground, making big patches on the bare dirt wherever gumbo soil was. I suppose that it furnished the salt for buffaloes in the days before they were killed off.

World War I and After

During World War I we were asked to plow and plant just as much as we could. Food would win the war, they said. We broke up prairie that had never been plowed before and planted wheat and grain, and made money for the first time. We kept this up until the depression began to hit us in 1928 and 1929. Every other homesteader west of the Missouri was doing the same thing. This was a mistake. The dry soil had no protection with the bunch grass gone. Winds picked up the loose dirt and piled it high around

107

buildings and fences and great clouds of dust filled the skies and were carried east. There was a story that went around about an old Indian who saw white men plowing up the prairie and sitting on his haunches, he picked up the dry dirt and sifted it between his fingers, saying, "Wrong side up." The homesteaders ruined the gama grasses that nature had worked at for centuries to hold that soil down. When the New Deal set up the Soil Conservation program, much of this land was taken out of cultivation. But the damages had been done and it took years to undo it.

Planting an Orchard

It took hard work and time but we did get an orchard started. After a childhood in southern Wisconsin, I just had to have fruit trees and flowers and shrubs around the house. My father who had a nursery at Sac City, Iowa, in 1913, sent out forty-eight apple trees to us, a few plums and cherries, and came out to help plant them. They grew wonderfully well the first year but the next year we had a deep snow that nearly covered the young trees. Hungry jackrabbits fed on the tops and killed most of them. A few came up from the roots but the best trees in the new orchard never made it. The gooseberries and strawberries did well when they did bear. When we picked wild currents, buffalo berries, and June berries, we had plenty for pies and sauce and for canning. But they would skip years so when we did have fruit, we made the best of it.

Prairie Flowers

In the spring the prairie was covered as far as the eye could see with a carpet of beautiful wild flowers. I had names for them but they were not the flower names found in books. Instead, I gave them the names of the tame flowers that they looked like. The first flower in the spring was the anemone which became the South Dakota State Flower. Then we had the little flower that made the ground white in the spring with its tiny petals. The yellow, blue, and white violets sprang up everywhere. There were the yucca, the gumbo lily, and another one that looked like the calla lily; the buffalo pea and the yellow and pink sweet william; snake root which we used for snake bite; wild roses that grew along the creek, buck brush and sun flowers that gave a flash of yellow and brown most everywhere; black-eyed susans, a blue flower that grew like a lady slipper, having many flowers, and there were yellow, pink, and other varieties. Even in dry years, the prairie was abloom in the early spring. Mother nature seemed to make every homesteader a bet: if we could survive the long, hard winter, she would give us wonderful wild flowers in the spring. Even in the summer, the alfalfa looked like an ocean of blue and green over the fields, and this, too, was one of the joys of living west of the Missouri.

Bees

One summer day I looked out over our alfalfa field and wondered if we wouldn't have better seed if we had bees to pollinate it. Besides, bees produce honey for sweetening. Right then I decided to get some bees. I had everything to learn about looking after them but it made sense to me that they would take care of themselves in the summertime when the alfalfa bloomed, so why not get some? We bought two swarms and it was not long until we had several hives. The table was furnished with honey for several years until the drought put us out of the bee business, and about everything else, too.

Our old dog, poor thing, learned to get along with bees early in life. He was in the habit of following me everywhere but one day conditions were not just right and the bees were ornery. They stung him from head to tail, and then took after me. Did they ever! I got stung from head to toe and looked as if I had warts all over. After that, I covered my face and hands and got along pretty well with them. The bees were like everything else. I had my finger in a lot of pies, but the main reason was more than just being curious about something; being a homesteader in a dry country and raising a family without too much help from Shy, I had to make every penny I could or we wouldn't have made it.

Wind Break

In 1912 when Shy came home from the Nebraska Sand Hills he wanted to set out a wind break around the yard. He had seen some native cedars used around some of the homesteads in the Sand Hills and liked them. All hands pitched in and dug big holes for the trees, and the next spring we took the team and went over to the Cheyenne River Breaks after the little cedars. We found all the trees we wanted — two feet high and well-shaped — wrapped the roots of each one in a wet gunny sack, hustled home with them, and put them in the holes. They never seemed to stop growing. Now we have a natural windbreak that slows up the blizzards that sweep across the prairies.

Gardening

It was the garden that kept us alive in the early years, and gave the family something more than beef to eat. I tried out all kinds of wild things and was surprised to find out what grew in South

109

Dakota. One year I planted artichokes. In the fall when we dug them we had sacks and sacks and I didn't know what to do with them. I fed them to the family but they didn't like them, so I put them in the slop pail for the hogs. The boys called this experiment a flop but the hogs seemed to go for the vegetable.

Then I tried wild peanuts and that was also a failure. But some of the little ground nuts produced wonderfully well. They were globules that grew on the end of the roots and were about the size of hazel nuts. We picked them like we would peanuts and found them good eating, but after awhile we got tired of them. When this soil had water, it would produce most anything, and sometimes just overdid itself. I once got started with stubbleberries. These little blue berries darn near took over my whole garden. The berries were delicious when made into pies and jams and I put up gallons of the sauce. It was not until the drought of 1934 that we got rid of them. By that time we'd had enough to do us the rest of our lives.

I always raised more garden than my family could use, so we helped supply the neighbors, too. One of our friends who didn't like to work in a garden brought over a bunch of seeds one spring and asked me to plant it in my garden for her. She wanted to feel free to come over and get things at any time. This seemed to be taking neighborliness too far, so I decided to cut back my garden to what my family needed and quit feeding all of Stanley County. I needed to spend my time on things that would bring in some money, not on things to give away. It was then that I turned to raising chickens.

But I enjoyed the garden even if it was a lot of work. The family all helped with the hoeing, but sometimes I found vegetables cut down and a row of weeds left standing. Shy always hoed down anything he didn't recognize. I always planted flowers in the garden so we could cut them and brighten up the house with them. One day Byron came in and said, "Mother, I think I've done a good job. I got all your pansies but one!" When the strawberries were ripe, the children practically lived in the strawberry bed and forgot about hoeing.

After we got the 4-H Club started, the boys had to have plots for their experiments. These plots had to be protected from the livestock and this was quite a problem. One year Byron had his ten-acre plot of corn east of the house. Louie Johnson's hogs kept getting out and coming down to the corn field and helping themselves. The businessmen at Philip had offered a $50 prize for the best corn crop produced by the 4-H boys, and so Byron's heart sank whenever Louie's hogs got in his plot and did a lot of damage yet Byron won the $25 second prize. When any of our hogs got out into Louie's field, he was always pretty mad, but if any of his hogs got in our fields, he would say, "Why, Mrs. Fairchild, my hogs didn't do you any damage. We got them out right away." This was the attitude of most of the homesteaders.

Our township decided to build a pond for watering livestock, but they hoped to make some money on the side with it. Homesteaders don't like cattlemen and sheepmen who let their stock roam loose around the country, jumping over fences and getting into the fields of corn or hay, with their owners never paying any damages. They thought the pond would solve the problem, and got quite a laugh out of taking people's stock and putting them into the corral there, holding them until damages were paid instead of taking them home or telling the owner that his stock was over in some homesteader's field. Since loose stock belonged to homesteaders as well as cattlemen and sheep ranchers, it didn't take long for the township to give up the idea of impounding cattle as a way of raising money.

From Homesteads to Bigger Farms

The country west of the Missouri had been changing ever since the homesteaders began to locate their claims. We were going from open range to fenced farms, from livestock only to mixed farming with both livestock and grain. The people leaving after the drought of 1911 had nothing to go on. They needed ready cash. The homesteaders who had quit the county left behind a lot of good grazing land, and so most of us branched out a little, began to cut the hay on this deserted land or put it into grain or other crops. The county bought various seeds and sold them to settlers, on time, but the seed was infested by the miserable bind weed and anyone getting that seed had his land ruined. We didn't buy any so we didn't ruin any of our land.

Selling Butter and Cream

After a few years, most of the ranchers had a milk cow or two, and some of us started a cooperative creamery. I bought a share although Shy thought it a foolish thing to do. We then got a cream separator, picked out our best cows, and began to milk and sell cream. Up to this time, I had made butter, packed it into jars, and sold it to any homesteader who came to the place after it. But that big old barrel churn that Shy had got for me was a bug-bear. The children hated to do the churning in it and I hated to wash it. It was too heavy to move around, but it did give us a lot of butter for our big family and for selling to neighbors and to the little stores around.

111

Frontier Woman

Little stores sprang up wherever there were enough homesteaders around to keep them going. Usually some farmer started one and ran it in a part of the house until he needed more shelves for the groceries he carried. There was usually a post office at the same place. I sold quite a lot of butter to these little "holes in the wall" until everybody began to milk a few cows. Then we began to sell cream to the cooperative creamery in Philip, taking turns hauling it into town. At one time we milked twenty-five cows. It was such a chore to milk the cows, run the milk through the separator, wash the separator twice a day, and keep the cream cool in crocks in the cellar until we took it to town. In the 1920's we put in a milking machine, and then the price of butterfat fell to twelve cents. Everything we had to sell went down. People drifted out of milking and began to raise beef cattle, and since Shy knew how to buy good stock, we always had good beeves around.

The homesteader who stayed west of the Missouri had to work harder and plan better than he would have had to do back in the Midwest where droughts and grasshoppers weren't such a problem. The droughts drove out many settlers and the rest of us bought their land at tax sales, added more livestock, and turned over more sod for grain and hay. We learned a lot from the 4-H Clubs' plots. If we hadn't learned "textbook farming" from these experiments and from the Ag college, we would have had to go back east, too.

Last Days on the Old Homestead

I suppose if I had known in 1898 what I know in 1950, I might never have left Wisconsin to take my first teaching job at Parker, South Dakota. At that time, the prospect of making $1200 a year instead of $800 or $900 teaching in a little red school house looked pretty good to me. Things look different when you are seventeen than they do when you are sixty-nine. I wouldn't have got married when I was eighteen and I wouldn't have married a widower who was forty-five and had a son as old as I was. But I did. I wouldn't have moved west of the Missouri with a husband who didn't have what it took to be a pioneer on the prairies. Shy was good-looking. People liked to talk to him, especially about horses. But he was as impractical as a man could be, and impractical people have no business pushing into the wilderness where only hard work and sacrifice make life possible. Over the years, Shy and I drifted farther apart. I finally decided it was up to me to make good on our South Dakota claim.

112

The ranch as it appeared in 1952

The Parting of the Ways

Over the years the rift between Shy and me deepened, and in 1930 we separated. We had a sale that year and divided up the property. He went to live by himself. He had always wanted to move to the Nebraska Sand Hills or to the Black Hills, but some freak of his nature caused him to build a little house within sight of the ranch, and there he batched alone a few years. Then he moved to Philip where he took a room. He came out to see Wayne and Clint, who lived near the home place, any time he wanted to come. In 1939, he got hurt in a poolroom brawl and from that time on he was never well. All his life he had complained about being sick, but I always thought it was in his head and that he was using this to get sympathy from me. I don't think he ever ran a fever and I know that he could always eat his meals.

When Shy and I separated in 1930, I gave myself five years to straighten out the indebtedness on the land, but never made it in that time. The depression and the drought made me stretch it out to ten years. In a lifetime, I had learned how to live with a mortgage but never really felt comfortable with one. By 1940, I had put together 1440 acres of land and had enough sheep and cattle to keep me out of the poor house, and then some. Though it was tough in the 1930's when prices were so low, I never went on relief. The relief workers told me that I couldn't get any help as long as I had eight cows and other livestock mortgage-free.

Wayne came to live with me after Shy moved out, and when he got married in 1936, he set up housekeeping on the Louis Johnson land north of the home place. He got a little start with sheep and cattle and settled down close to home, the only one of the eight children who decided to stay with the old homestead west of the Missouri.

After Shy got hurt in the brawl in Philip, the boys brought him back to the home place where he stayed most of his remaining days. When he got worse, Clint and Wayne took him to the hospital in Pierre. Dr. Riggs said he had pneumonia, and gave him sulfa drugs. He didn't respond and this puzzled the doctor. Age may have had something to do with it. The boys sent for me and I went to the hospital to see him. I saw at once that Shy was up to his old tricks and acting contrary as usual. He was taking the sulfa pills out of his mouth when the nurse left the room. I called the nurse and told her what he was doing. She gave him the medicine in another form. But it was too late. The doctor told me that his time had come and that I should let the family know that the end was near. Shy crossed his last divide on May 7, 1940 at the age of eighty-six. I hope that he found a pretty homestead over there, with plenty of hot-blooded horses and country fairs, enough to pleasure him through all the years of eternity. With him I had made my bed, and I had also slept in it. I only wanted a bigger dream than he did — on the South Dakota frontier.

"The old Sioux chief said he could tell us how many snowfalls we would have. You take the day of the month of the first snow deep enough to track a cat, add the age of the moon, and that gives you the number of snows for the winter."

"It was so cold that when he died they just sharpened his feet and drove him into the ground."

"When the chinook hit South Dakota melting the snow, the old settler kept his team on a dead run and still could keep only the front runners of his sled on the snow."